Effective Schools and Classrooms:

A Research-Based Perspective

David A. Squires
William G. Huitt
John K. Segars

Association for Supervision and
Curriculum Development
225 North Washington Street
Alexandria, Virginia 22314

Price: $7.50
ASCD Stock Number: 611-83298
ISBN: 0-87120-119-4
Library of Congress Card Catalog Number: 83-71147

Editing:
Ronald S. Brandt, ASCD Executive Editor
Sally Banks Zakariya, Managing Editor, Booklets

Cover design:
William J. Kircher and Associates

This work was partially supported through funds from the National Institute
of Education, Department of Education. The opinions expressed herein do not
necessarily reflect the positions or policy of NIE or of ASCD, and no official
endorsement by NIE or ASCD should be inferred.

Contents

Foreword

Why is it that so many seemingly effective school practices never become truly effective school practices? Is it because the research is couched in obtuse language? Is it because the research does not filter down to the practitioner? Is it because the practitioner is more concerned with the pragmatics than with the theory?

Effective Schools and Classrooms: A Research-Based Perspective makes an unusually lucid attempt to clarify these questions. The book has an overriding theme of improving student achievement. Its authors—David Squires, William Huitt, and John Segars—combine the research on effective classrooms with the research on effective schools to suggest important ways that teachers and administrators can make a difference in student achievement.

In a clearly written, carefully documented work, Squires, Huitt, and Segars examine those factors that are most closely related to achievement. They describe how a school's organization, personnel, and climate affect achievement. And finally, they indicate how principals, superintendents, and school boards can use this information to improve schools.

LAWRENCE S. FINKEL
President, 1983–84
Association for Supervision and
Curriculum Development

Acknowledgments

Many people and organizations make a book like this possible. Research for Better Schools, Inc. (RBS), supported in part by the National Institute of Education, housed our work and to a large extent provided the time and stimulation that helped us formulate our ideas. Our thanks to the RBS management: John Hopkins, Lou Maguire, and Skip McCann. David Helms, Anne Graber, and other members of the Basic Skills Project at RBS helped us test these ideas and their meaning for those who administer and teach in schools. Janet Caldwell was especially helpful in writing the chapter on effective classrooms. Ron Brandt and the editorial committee of ASCD were enthusiastic and encouraged our endeavors. Superintendent Joan D. Abrams and the School Board of Red Bank Borough, New Jersey, also lent their support to our efforts.

For preparation of the many drafts, our deep gratitude to Ullik Rouk for her editorial assistance and to Fran Shelkin, Doris Harris, and Kathy Hourigan, whose patience and secretarial skills we all applaud.

For our families, who endured our trials and exalted in our successes, our love.

1.

Improving Classrooms and

Schools: What's Important

"Our student achievement has improved!" Bill, an elementary school principal, bubbled with enthusiasm. He had just received the results of his school's standardized achievement tests, and, after three years of hard work, the outcome was gratifying. Here's a part of his story:

Three years ago, I accepted my second principalship in a 400-student elementary school that had a history of low scores on achievement tests. Most students left the school at the end of fifth grade a year behind in math and reading. Many were two and three years behind. The students came from poor families, and while a good many staff members worked conscientiously, a consensus had developed that not much more could be expected of "our" students.

"Our" students are now scoring above grade level in reading and math. That's a fact I'm very proud of. The teachers have worked hard to achieve this change. Let me summarize what we've done in three years.

During the first year, the staff and I took a close look at our achievement history and the kinds of skills and knowledge required by the achievement tests. We tried to determine if we were systematically teaching the skills that were tested. We found, to some people's surprise, that we weren't. The faculty decided to develop units in both reading and math that specifically addressed these skills and provided an opportunity for students to learn.

In addition, I spent much of my time in classrooms making sure students were involved in their learning. About a half-dozen teachers were having problems with classroom management, and students tended not to be involved. We worked through the problems using a cycle of supervision that I introduced at a couple of faculty meetings. While the supervision was not always comfortable, we were able to get more students involved.

During the second year, we continued writing our skill units. I noticed that students in many classrooms were consistently failing many of these units, however. Indeed, the failure rate at the end of the first year had been high. A committee of teachers decided the school should adopt a mastery learning approach to instruction. This approach gives students who fail the first "formative test" more instruction in the skill area and a chance to succeed on the final test. We found that by providing the extra instruction, many more students were able to pass the "mastery" or final tests for each unit. Students were experiencing a higher level of success. Even grades on report cards went up. I also began to ask all teachers to report their mastery test scores to me after each unit so I can keep current track of student progress.

In the third year, we further developed a supervisory system that involved assisting teachers in planning, instruction, and classroom management. We also continued to look at students' involvement in classroom activities and at their success on the skill units.

These few activities have helped give the school an academic focus. Student achievement has improved consistently at all grade levels in the first three years. In addition, we also worked on school procedures so the school is more orderly now. And, most important, teachers are expecting, and getting, more success from students.

The ideas we put into practice exemplify the important areas highlighted by research on improving student achievement. In fact, I was hired partly for my use of ideas identified by the research on effective classrooms and schools. These ideas seem to me to be good common sense. For example, a school should be a safe place, physically and psychologically, for children to engage in the interesting pursuit of learning, in a climate where everyone succeeds. Running a safe school means providing a few clear rules and then making sure they're enforced with an even hand. Learning needs to be first, and teachers need to help provide children with exciting experiences that maintain high student involvement and interest. All students should master academic skills. When teachers agree on what all students should learn, then student achievement is likely to improve and everyone is more likely to succeed.

The principal is one of the most important people in the school when it comes to setting school climate and providing leadership. The principal makes sure the staff has the supervision needed to support professional improvement. Through supervision, teachers are aware of how their planning, instruction, and management patterns affect their students and their students' achievement.

This principal's report summarizes the findings of recent research on the characteristics of effective classrooms and schools. The purpose of this book is to use research findings like these to suggest areas of improvement with the aim of improving student achievement. Along the way, we'll provide examples of how teachers and administrators have used these ideas to improve classrooms and schools. In this chapter, we describe how we picture the influences that foster student achievement on standardized tests, and summarize our understandings about student achievement.

Over the past 20 years, we've learned some things about student achievement and instruction in schools:

- Student achievement can be measured with validity and reliability in important areas.
- Teachers and schools make a difference in how well students succeed on standardized tests.
- Students who are involved in class generally succeed better than those who don't pay attention.
- Students who succeed on daily assignments and tests are more likely to have higher achievement on standardized tests.
- When teachers teach most of the content and skills covered by standardized tests, students are likely to have higher achievement scores.
- Curriculum packages, in and of themselves, will not result in higher achievement for students.
- Schools can produce exceptional student achievement, even when students come from low socioeconomic backgrounds.
- The principal exerts a tremendous influence toward refining and maintaining a school's social system that promotes achievement and discipline.
- Change in school practices happens over a number of years.

These statements don't appear too startling, but then neither do other common-sense notions, such as the idea that the more training teachers receive, the better they will perform—an idea that, unfortunately, is not supported by recent studies. But the preceding list of learnings, because each one is borne out by research, provides us with some reliable and valid places to start when we are trying to improve schools and classrooms.

A caution is in order, however. There are to date relatively few experimental studies demonstrating that a change in any combination of these characteristics results in a change in student achievement on standardized tests. We are nevertheless encouraged by the depth and breadth of the mostly correlational studies that provided the foundation for this book. Taken as a whole, they suggest important areas to consider if improved student achievement is the goal.

A Model for School and Classroom Effectiveness

We have combined research on effective classrooms with research on

Figure 1. A Model for Improving School and Classroom Effectiveness.

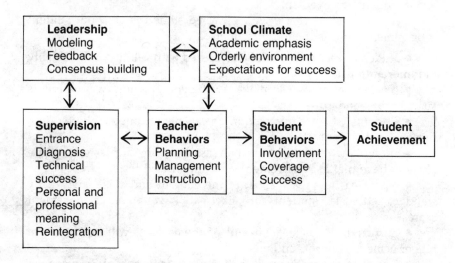

effective schools to suggest important ways that teachers and administrators make a difference in student achievement (Squires, Huitt, and Segars, 1981). Our model, shown in Figure 1, provides one way of viewing schools and classrooms in order to answer the question, "What can schools do to improve student achievement?" In constructing this model, we begin by suggesting those factors most closely related to achievement, and we build the model outward to show how the school's organization—that is, its personnel (such as teachers and supervisors), administrative leadership, and school climate—affect student achievement. The following discussion of the elements of the model will proceed in the same order as its construction.

Effective Classrooms

Not surprisingly, student behavior—or what students do in class—is most directly correlated with their achievement scores. Specifically, research points to three areas that have the most potential for affecting student achievement:

1. **Involvement:** the amount of time a student actively works on academic content

2. **Coverage:** the amount of content covered by a student during a year, especially content tested by a standardized instrument

3. **Success:** how well students perform on daily assignments and unit tests indicating mastery of academic content.

Student involvement, coverage, and success make sense: if students have successfully spent enough time covering the content to be tested, then achievement should be high. We propose that measures of involvement (or engagement), coverage, and success become the focus of school improvement efforts. Such measures could be used on a quarterly basis in evaluating a school's progress toward improved achievement. Involvement, coverage, and success are so important and so relatively easy to measure that they should be carefully accounted for, much as money spent to support the school is accounted for. Chapter Two suggests how this can be accomplished by centering the school's program around improving students' involvement, increasing coverage of content, and promoting student success.

Student behaviors and student achievement—the last two elements of the model in Figure 1—are thus the starting points for the model. The rest of the model proposes school organization that supports the all-important student behaviors of involvement, success, and coverage.

The next element is teacher behavior. Teachers have the most influence over student behavior and support student achievement through planning, instruction, and classroom management. To the extent that the teachers' behaviors support students' involvement, success, and coverage, then student achievement will improve. Teachers can do this through planning, delivering instruction, and managing student behavior in their classrooms. If improved student achievement is the goal, then research has some suggestions about which teacher behavior patterns are most effective.

Just as a teacher's behavior supports students' behaviors, so supervision can support teachers. A positive supervisory process that brings to light the conflicts inherent in any supervisory relationship may promote professional growth if the supervision is focused on improving the students' involvement, coverage, and success.

Supervision also creates the opportunity for increasing teachers' skills in planning, managing, and delivering instruction. In the process of supervision, the supervisor and the teacher explore the meanings in the patterns of their professional behavior. The goal of positive supervision is to improve professional practice so that both supervisor and teacher become increasingly competent in performing their roles. If the teacher and the supervisor agree that student achievement is important, then patterns of student and teacher behavior are an appropriate focus of supervision.

Effective Schools

In unusually effective schools, active leadership creates a school climate in which success is expected, academics are emphasized, and the environment is orderly.

Teachers and administrators in these schools emphasize a curriculum of reading, writing, and math in a businesslike environment that promotes and reinforces disciplined instruction that takes up much of the school day. Teachers in effective schools spend more time on lessons (beginning and ending on time) and provide periods of quiet work. In secondary schools, homework is given and graded regularly. Thus, an academic emphasis promotes student involvement and coverage.

Students cannot be successfully engaged in academic work in a disorderly environment, however. Effective schools generally recognize a uniform standard of discipline, which is enforced fairly by administrators and teachers. Students are encouraged to hold positions of responsibility, and their contributions are publicly recognized. Classroom routines also promote an orderly environment in which lessons start and end on time, students bring the necessary materials to class, and teachers give and correct homework. Students are more likely to be engaged if classroom routines and discipline procedures help keep them on task and involved.

In effective schools, students are expected to reach the goals set for them. Student success is built into lessons, and teachers provide consistent rewards for demonstrated achievement. Standards for achievement in effective schools are high, yet reasonable, and students expect to master their academic work and graduate from high school. They feel teachers care about their academic performance and believe hard work is more important to that performance than luck. Because they have been successful in the past, the students have a sense of control over their environment.

Student success is clearly related to school climate, which is, in turn, related to leadership. Three leadership processes build and maintain a school's climate: modeling, feedback, and consensus building. Leadership generally comes from the principal, although teachers may provide it as well. Principals, in particular, model appropriate behavior, which supports a positive school climate. Principals support inservice programs, monitor classrooms and supervise instruction, and provide time for teachers to plan together. By doing so, they set the tone and focus of the school. Even paying attention to faculty punctuality reinforces the principal's concern for how school time is spent. But principals can also provide negative models. If the principal believes students are not likely to learn, then the principal is not likely to be concerned about whether the staff devotes enough time to instruction.

Feedback that supports and recognizes successful academic performance and appropriate behavior is also more likely to occur in effective schools. Principals give teachers feedback by observing class-rooms, conferring with teachers about instructional issues, and providing inservice to enhance teachers' skills. They see that formal punishments are administered swiftly, and they monitor the faculty to reduce verbal humiliation and unsanctioned violence against students. In short, the principal's actions communicate the message that praise, rewards, and encouragements need to outweigh negative sanctions.

Developing consensus about academic focus and expectations for behavior is a third leadership process in effective schools. Consensus is generated by schoolwide projects for change and by appropriate and consistent models and feedback. Again, the principal is pivotal in developing this consensus. Principals of effective schools have a focus in mind when running their schools. They ensure that school goals are set, guide the development of consensus around those goals, and systematically check to see that the school is operating accordingly. In schools where students and faculty perceive a consensus on discipline and academics, school outcomes are generally high.

Measuring Student Achievement

Our model focuses on factors associated with student achievement on standardized tests—an important educational outcome. Standardized tests provide a reliable and valid indicator of school outcomes, particularly in the basic skills areas of reading comprehension and mathematics computation.

While schools certainly have other purposes and goals as well, if they aren't successful in teaching most of their students these basic skills, then they probably will not be considered successful by students, parents, and the school board. To be sure, testing doesn't tell the whole story, nor is it the only valued result of education. Indeed, some skills—such as writing, oral language skills, and group problem solving—are difficult to assess with traditional standardized instruments, but that does not mean they should be ignored as important outcomes or significant parts of the curriculum. We use standardized tests as benchmarks for a school's success because they are more reliable, valid, and accepted than any other outcome measure. With that in mind, let's take a look at some of the things we know about student achievement and standardized testing.

First, student achievement on standardized tests generally predicts achievement for succeeding years, and gains or deficits in standardized tests tend to have a cumulative effect when viewed across a number of years. Thus, the difference in achievement between the top and bottom students increases with their ages. Predictive validity of standardized scores, and their correlation with future achievement, support their importance as a significant outcome measure.

Second, as the public furor over the decline of SAT scores during the 1970s clearly showed, standardized tests provide a measure of educational effectiveness in the public's eyes. Indeed, many minimum competency testing and school improvement programs have resulted from public concern for falling scores and demands in the state legislature for educational accountability. Because of public acceptance, then, standardized tests are an important measure of educational outcomes.

Third, schools that achieve above expectations on standardized tests also tend to succeed in other important areas, such as attendance, student self-concept and participation, lack of student disruption and vandalism, and low incidence of delinquent behavior in the community. This suggests that areas that correlate with standardized test performance provide clues to more effective classrooms and schools. For these reasons, our model organizes correlates of student achievement from many studies to suggest areas schools can change in order to increase student achievement.

Overview

The model provides the outline for this book. In Chapter 2, we provide an overview of research about involvement, coverage, and success. Instruments and procedures for monitoring these student behaviors are included in Appendix 1. We then describe how teachers' behaviors in the classroom support these variables for improved student achievement and suggest implications for action based on the research.

Chapter 3 suggests ways administrators can help teachers promote involvement, coverage, and success through positive supervision in which conflicts inherent in supervision are appropriately managed so professional growth can occur. Bill, the principal introduced at the beginning of this chapter, gives an example of his supervisory system.

Unusually effective schools are the topic of Chapter 4, and Chapter 5 demonstrates how indicators of effective schools are grouped into the more general categories of school climate and leadership.

In Chapter 6, a hypothetical case study is used to show how Bill's school leadership processes promoted a school climate where there is an academic emphasis, an orderly environment, and expectations for success. The chapter ends with suggestions for superintendents and school boards who want improved student achievement. Chapter 7 includes a questionnaire for collecting data about a school's effectiveness. The book concludes by summarizing ideas about change in schools.

2.

Characteristics of

Effective Classrooms

"There's so much research it often seems contradictory. I just can't figure out what's important and what isn't."

"I don't see how research can help improve my teaching—it's all too vague and too abstract."

Teachers and administrators alike seem to want to be guided by the best we know about teaching and learning, but they often have reservations like those quoted above. Fortunately, research has provided some cues as to what is important when attempting to improve classroom practice, especially as it relates to student achievement in the basic skills of reading, language arts, and mathematics. Figure 1 summarizes many of those findings. The purpose of this chapter is to present some of those findings and suggest how several key indicators of effective classrooms can be monitored by teachers and administrators.

One important finding is that students' classroom behavior is the most direct link to student achievement. A second important finding is that teachers' behavior can affect students' behavior in ways that will lead to improved student learning.

An overview of the effective classroom research indicates that students do better on standardized achievement tests in basic skills when they have been actively involved in and successful on content for which they are academically prepared and which is closely related to the content tested.

The same research indicates there are few single teacher behaviors that seem to be critical in and of themselves. Looking at composites of important teacher behaviors, however, we seem to find three categories:

9

Figure 1. Dimensions of Classroom Effectiveness.

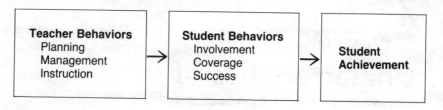

(1) planning, or getting ready for classroom activities; (2) management, which has to do with controlling students' behavior; and (3) instruction, which concerns providing for or guiding students' learning. Teachers who plan, manage, and instruct in ways that facilitate student involvement, coverage, and success are likely to be considered more effective.

These findings may not sound very new or surprising; in fact, many educators could probably identify these same student and teacher behaviors simply from experience. But the fact is, this knowledge is being applied in a wide variety of ways in school systems across the country. And if we look carefully at the research, there are a few surprises.

Student Behavior

The important student behaviors of involvement, coverage, and success have been studied independently and show a significant relationship to student achievement.

Involvement

Involvement simply means the amount of time the student spends actively involved in learning a specific subject matter. Involvement has two aspects: how much time is provided by the teacher (allocated time), and how well students are engaged during the time provided (engagement rate). Student engaged time, or time-on-task, is a measure of involvement that takes into consideration both allocated time and engagement rate (that is, student engaged time = allocated time × engagement rate).

One of the surprises that research on time has provided is the range that exists in practice for both allocated time and engagement rate. For example, Dishaw (1977) reported that time allocated per day for second-grade reading and language arts ranged from a low of 34 minutes to a high of 127 minutes; for second-grade math, the range was from 30 minutes to 59 minutes. Similarly, allocated time for fifth-grade reading and language arts ranged from 57 minutes to 156 minutes and for fifth-grade math, 23 minutes to 76 minutes. Ranges among classrooms for engagement rate are similar to those for allocated time—namely, in some classrooms, students are engaged an average of 30 percent of the time, while in others the average is 90 percent (Brady, Clinton, Sweeney, Peterson, and Poynor, 1977).

A second surprise in the time research, given the average allocated time and engagement rate found in other studies, was the amount of student engaged time needed before one could expect improved student achievement. For example, it would be reasonable to expect an average classroom to have about 72 minutes of student engaged time in reading/language arts and 27 minutes in math,[1] but a reanalysis of the Stallings and Kaskowitz (1974) Follow Through Evaluation Study indicated that much more student engaged time is needed (Rim, Caldwell, Helms, and Huitt, 1980). In a first-grade classroom, as much as 130 to 210 minutes of student engaged time in reading and language arts may be needed to show greater-than-expected student achievement gains in that subject (based on a pretest), whereas in a fifth-grade classroom, only 90 to 135 minutes of student engaged time in reading and language arts may be needed (see Figure 2).

A third surprise is that more time isn't always better. For example, the same reanalysis of the Stallings and Kaskowitz data (Rim, Caldwell, Helms, and Huitt, 1980) showed that for first-grade mathematics, student achievement increased as student engaged time increased up to about 95 minutes per day, but then began to *decrease* as more student engaged time was accumulated (see Figure 2). Similar results were found for third-grade reading and language arts: approximately 135 minutes of student engaged time appeared to be optimal.

Coverage

Coverage, the appropriateness of the content covered by the student, can be considered in two ways. First, is the content covered appropriate given the student's prior learning? And second, is it appropriate given the achievement test the school or district will use to judge student achievement?

The issue of prior learning is relatively simple: does the student, before instruction begins, exhibit the prerequisites necessary to learn the new material? For example, students should be able to add two-digit numbers without regrouping before we teach them how to add two-

---

[1] This figure is based on an average allocated time of 120 minutes and 45 minutes in reading/language arts and mathematics, respectively (Heinrichs and Rim, 1980; Graeber, Rim, and Unka, 1977), and an average engagement rate of 60 percent in both subjects (Brady et al., 1977).

Figure 2. Relationship of Student Engaged Time in Reading/Language Arts and Mathematics to Student Achievement.

Subject	Student Engaged Time (minutes/day)		
Reading/Language Arts	Below Expected	At Expected	Above Expected
Grade 1	40–110	110–130	130–210
3	45–90	90–115	115–135[a]
5	40–80	80–90	90–135
Mathematics			
Grade 1	5–35	35–45	45–95[a]
3	10–45	45–60	60–100
5		Range = 15–45[b]	

[a]Student achievement beyond this point began to decrease as student engaged time increased (maximum value: third-grade R/LA = 170; first-grade math = 140).
[b]Not significantly related to student achievement.

digit numbers with regrouping. On a broader scale, most of the content taught in school assumes some developmental sequence of learning tasks. It is generally assumed that a student needs to learn first-grade content before attempting second-grade content, that a student should pass Algebra I before beginning Algebra II, and so on. It is often easier for teachers to assume that all students entering a learning situation have the necessary prerequisites, but student test results, grades, and cumulative records provide abundant evidence that each student entering a classroom brings a unique array of knowledge and skills.

Bloom (1976) reviews research that highlights the importance of attending to students' prior learning. As much as 80 percent of the variance in post-test scores may be accounted for by pretest scores alone. Similarly, Bracht and Hopkins (1972) found that about two-thirds of the variance in eleventh-grade achievement could be predicted from third-grade achievement. The knowledge the student brings to the learning situation, then, has a strong effect on how well the student performs on subsequent measures of student learning. Unless low-scoring students are given instruction that takes into account what they currently know and can do, their pattern of achievement is unlikely to change.

The second aspect of coverage—the extent to which the content covered by the students is the content assessed by district achievement tests—is sometimes referred to as criterion-related instruction or instructional overlap. As one might expect, students in classes that cover more of the content tested generally make greater gains in achievement. In fact, in one study (Brady et al., 1977), achievement gains were more highly linked to the differences in instructional overlap than to any other classroom variable.

A surprise is the range of criterion-related content actually covered during instruction. In the Instructional Dimensions Study, a study of reading/language arts and mathematics instruction involving over 100 first- and 100 third-grade teachers (Brady et al., 1977), the researchers found that the percent of overlap between content taught and content tested on a norm-referenced achievement test ranged from 4 to 95 percent. That is, students in some classrooms covered an average of only 4 percent of the content tested, while students in other classrooms covered an average of 95 percent.

A second surprise is that the percent of instructional overlap for which one would predict better-than-expected achievement (again based on a pretest) was found to be different for reading/language arts than for mathematics. And, at least for mathematics, the level of overlap also depended on grade level. For reading/language arts, about 70 percent of the content tested needed to be actually covered during instruction before one would predict that students would make better-than-expected achievement gains. For mathematics, on the other hand, the comparable figures were 40 percent for first grade and 60 percent for third grade (Brady et al., 1977). In other words, if teachers want student scores on an achievement test to be better than might be expected on the basis of a pretest, their elementary (first- and third-grade) students should cover at least 70 percent of the content represented on the reading/language arts achievement test, and at least 40 percent of the first-grade and 60 percent of the third-grade mathematics content tested.

A third surprise is that, again, more is not always better—at least not for first-grade mathematics, in which student achievement increases as instructional overlap increases up to about 65 percent, but decreases when instructional overlap exceeds that level (Brady et al., 1977). That is, covering *more* than 65 percent of the content represented by items on the first-grade mathematics test seems to have a detrimental effect on student achievement, at least on the standardized test used in the study.

Success

Success refers to the extent to which students accurately complete the assignments they have been given. Bloom (1976) and Skinner (1968) consider student success to be one of the most important of all instructional variables. Followers of Skinner's theory, in fact, advocate "errorless learning," suggesting that learning proceeds optimally when no errors are made.

By now the first surprise for success should no longer be a surprise. As is the case for both involvement and coverage, the range for students' success is quite large. For example, in the Beginning Teacher Evaluation Study, Phase III (BTES-III), researchers found that students in some second-grade classrooms had completed as few as 9 percent of their reading tasks with no errors or only careless ones (i.e., at high success), while other students completed as many as 88 percent of their reading tasks at high success (Fisher, Filby, Marliave, Cahen, Dishaw, Moore, and Berliner, 1978). Comparable ranges were found for second-grade mathematics (2 to 92 percent), fifth-grade reading (15 to 81 percent), and fifth-grade mathematics (8 to 89 percent).

The second surprise is that the appropriate percent of high success seems to contradict Skinner's "errorless learning" theory. For example, in a reanalysis of the Fisher et al. (1978) data, Rim (1980) found that student achievement in second-grade reading increased as the proportion of tasks completed at high success increased up to about 75 percent, but then began to *decrease* as more tasks were covered at a high success rate. A study of 43 second- and third-grade classrooms (Crawford, King, Brophy, and Evertson, 1975) somewhat corroborates the work of Fisher et al. (1978). These investigators found that the optimal level of correct answers to teachers' oral questions was around 75 percent, again considerably different from the 100 percent hypothesized by Skinner.

The third surprise related to the research on success is that the appropriate level of success may vary depending on student characteristics. For example, using highly structured programmed materials and experimentally varying success rates, Crawford (1978) found that college students classified as having low motivation for achievement but high fear of failure did best when their success rate was approximately 93 percent and worst when their success rate was approximately 60 percent. Conversely, students classified as having high motivation for achievement and low fear of failure performed optimally at a 60 percent success rate and did worst at a 93 percent rate.

Summary

To summarize, the research on involvement, coverage, and success indicates that wide ranges for these behaviors are found in current practice; that more is not always better; that the appropriate levels may depend on grade level, subject area, and student characteristics; and that the appropriate levels are different from what we might expect on the basis of current practice.

Taken independently, these behaviors can be considered critical aspects of student classroom behavior. Combined, as Fisher and his colleagues (1978) have done, they form the construct of Academic Learning Time (ALT). ALT is defined as the amount of time that students spend actively working on criterion-related content at a high rate of success. It is instructive to look at how much ALT students actually accumulate per day, given that students generally spend about five hours per day in school (Brady et al., 1977). Data from the BTES-III study indicate that second-grade students accumulated about 11 minutes Academic Learning Time a day for mathematics and about 19 minutes for reading. Average ALT for fifth-grade students was only slightly better: about 14 minutes a day for mathematics and about 35 minutes for reading. Again, however, there are wide variations among classrooms. For example, some second-grade students spent an average of only 3 minutes a day working successfully on reading, while others spent as much as 42 minutes. Certainly, there is room for improvement in most classrooms in terms of these critical student behaviors.

Teacher Behavior

Our review of the research on effective classrooms indicates that teachers can have an impact on student behavior and student achievement. And teachers do that by planning, managing, and instructing in ways that keep students involved and successfully covering appropriate content.

Planning

A number of models of teacher planning describe planning as a process of selecting objectives, diagnosing learner characteristics, and selecting appropriate instructional and management strategies (Peterson, Marx, and Clark, 1978). Many teachers do not consider these aspects during the planning process, however. They are more likely to focus primarily on tasks or activities that will be presented in the classroom, rather than on instructional objectives (e.g., Peterson et al., 1978; Shavelson and Stern, 1981; Zahorik, 1975).

Nevertheless, if students' involvement, coverage, and success are to be adequate, careful planning will certainly play a significant role. For example, selecting appropriate management and instructional strategies is likely to keep students more involved. Likewise, there is reason to believe that planning to cover skills and objectives that are to be tested will increase the overlap between content taught and content tested. Also, considering such student characteristics as prior learning in the selection of appropriate instructional strategies is likely to lead to better student success.

Prior learning. A number of Bloom's students (Anderson, 1973; Arlin, 1973; Block, 1970; Levin, 1975; and Ozecelik, 1974) have shown that if deficiencies in prior learning are attended to, most students can learn what was previously learned by only the best students. Most of these studies involved comparing scores from one group of students who received corrective procedures after each learning task with scores from a group of students who did not. For the group whose prior learning was attended to, the correlation between entering and ending achievement was .36, while it was .68 for the other group. This means, then, that by attending to prior learning (that is, by altering the "normal" instructional sequence), teachers were able to reduce the effect of students' entering achievement on their final achievement.

The work of Bloom and his students suggests that some method of identifying and attending to students' knowledge of prerequisite skills is a vital aspect of classroom instruction. Bloom summarizes his position as follows:

If the school can assure each learner of a history of adequate cognitive entry in the first two or three years of the elementary school period, the student's subsequent history of learning in the school is likely to be more positive with respect to both cognitive and affective learning outcomes. Similarly, for each *new set* of learning experiences which start at later stages of the school program (e.g., science, social studies, mathematics, second language), providing for adequate achievement and appropriate cognitive entry behavior in the initial and early stages of the new set of learning experiences is likely to have a strong positive effect on the learning of the later sets of tasks in the series (1976, p. 70).

One method of attending to students' prior learning is by carefully examining students' previous achievement test results. To get a rough idea of how a student or group of students stands in relation to national and local norms, the teacher can look at percentile rankings, stanine scores, grade equivalent scores, or similar ratings. For more specific information, the teacher can look at the right response summary provided for most tests, which will indicate why a specific score was received.

A second way is to give a short quiz on knowledge pertinent to the next lesson. Of course we have all heard stories of teachers who tested more than they taught, but sometimes just two or three questions can elicit the required information. However, sometimes it is simply easier and quicker to give a brief review before introducing new content.

Instructional overlap. Planning the content to be taught so that it overlaps adequately with the content tested is not an easy matter. Often the teacher is provided with a curriculum guide that defines the content to be taught and a text that supposedly covers the same content. In addition, teachers must consider their own opinions, as well as those of the principal and parents, as to which topics are of most importance. Consequently, the teacher is likely to need some help and support in selecting content to be taught if an adequate instructional overlap is to be obtained.

One way districts or individual schools might help is by developing a curriculum guide that at least represents the majority of the content to be tested. This will likely require some adjustments in the present guide (if one has already been developed), since finding a test that overlaps with the content and skills in the curriculum guide is difficult, if not impossible. Also, tests vary widely in the emphasis on various topics, even when the content covered is the same. For example, in a study of fourth-grade mathematics tests, the proportion of items using whole numbers varied from 39 percent on one test to 66 percent on another (Floden, Porter, Schmidt, and Freeman, 1980).

One drawback to relying on a curriculum guide is that teachers may not follow the guide when planning what content to teach (English, 1980). Indeed, teachers are sometimes more likely to be influenced by content covered in the selected text than in the guide (Floden, Porter, Schmidt, Freeman, and Schwille, 1980). For that reason, a second alternative might be to select a text that overlaps well with the test. However, there is a wide variety of topics covered by texts and tests, and again, an adequate overlap may be difficult. For example, in a study of core topics covered in fourth-grade mathematics texts and tests, only six specific areas were consistently emphasized across the three text-books and the five tests considered (Freeman and Kuhns, 1980). In fact, this same study showed that, at best, only 41 percent of the tested topics were covered by one of the textbooks.

Given that teachers would likely need to teach additional topics if an adequate overlap is to be obtained, and given teachers' apparent unwillingness to omit topics already being taught (Floden et al., 1980), any effort to improve overlap will probably require considerable reflection as to what is most important. While this could be a time-consuming and conflict-laden process, there is little reason to believe that any improvement would be made unless it is done in a systematic way.

Management

The second category of teacher behavior to be considered is management, commonly called classroom management. This category includes all the skills and techniques that are primarily intended to control students' behavior and are consequently most relevant when attempting to increase students' academic involvement.

A number of recent studies on classroom organization and effective teaching by the Research and Development Center for Teacher Education (Anderson, Evertson, and Emmer, 1979; Emmer and Evertson, 1980; Emmer, Evertson, and Anderson, 1980) provide support for reviews of earlier work (for example, Kounin, 1977; Duke, 1979). Several broad themes have emerged from this research, including the need to:

• Analyze the tasks of the first few weeks in detail and predict what will confuse or distract students

• Present rules, procedures, expectations, and assignments to students in a clear, detailed manner and establish classroom routines

• Establish a system of student accountability for behavior and academic work

• Consistently monitor behavior and work and provide feedback on its appropriateness.

Other effective classroom management strategies are (1) structuring the physical environment to prevent distractions (Berliner, 1978); (2) planning smooth transitions between activities (Arlin, 1979); (3) pacing activities so that students become neither confused nor bored (Fisher et al., 1978; Kounin and Doyle, 1975); and (4) avoiding negative affect when controlling students' behavior (Soar and Soar, 1977).

Teachers we have worked with have reported that they could increase student involvement by making very simple changes in their management strategies. For example, some teachers simply print an independent work assignment on the board before students enter class, so that students can start working immediately. Others give students flags so they can signal the teacher when a problem develops during seatwork, rather than stopping and waiting for the teacher's help. Still others ask students to keep a book at their desks so they can read when they have completed the assigned work.

We have found it helpful for teachers to work in pairs or small groups as they attempt to develop specific management strategies in their classrooms. A striking example of how this can work is the case of a relatively inexperienced elementary teacher who asked an older, more experienced colleague to come into her room and observe her students' involvement. During the observation, it became readily apparent that, during small group activities, as many as seven or eight students would be out of the room (in the restroom, they said) at any one time.

As the two teachers discussed the situation, the younger teacher said, "Yes, I had noticed the situation. But the students really do need to go to the restroom, and I thought it unreasonable to not let anyone go." The teacher then decided to try a strategy that was suggested by the observer. She took two pieces of cardboard, labeled one "boys" and the other "girls," and hung them up in the back of the room. She then told the children, "Only one person can leave the room at a time. When you go out, simply turn the card over so that the blank side is showing; when you come back, return the card to its original position. If the blank side is showing when you want to go to the restroom, you must wait until the other student returns."

When the observer returned several days later for another observation, she reported a dramatic change. The children had quickly adapted to the new routine and were no longer leaving the room en masse. The result was higher student involvement.

One last note about management strategies. Several studies (Duckett, Parke, Clark, McCarthy, Lotto, Gregory, Herling, and Burlson, 1980; Goldstein and Weber, 1981) show that the most effective approaches to management build group cohesiveness and consensus, establish an academic emphasis, and develop positive teacher-student and student-student relationships. An authoritarian approach in which the teacher assumes full responsibility for controlling student behavior, often through the use of pressure and force, is significantly less effective.

Instruction

The third category of teacher behavior is instruction, often called the quality of instruction or the process of instruction. Typically, research on specific instructional methodologies (such as questioning strategies or encouraging pupil participation) reveal numerous and complex relationships with student achievement (Rosenshine and Furst, 1963; Medley, 1977). Several efforts have been made to synthesize research on classroom characteristics and instructional methods, however. These efforts range from theoretical models, such as those of Leinhardt (1978, 1980), to prescriptive models, such as direct instruction (Rosenshine, 1977, 1979; Good and Grouws, 1979) and mastery learning (Anderson and Block, 1977; Bloom, 1976; Block and Burns, 1976; Burns, 1979; Barber, 1979; Abrams, 1979).[2] These instructional models, in addition to other syntheses of research on classroom instruction (Hunter, 1979; Medley, 1977), point to a number of behaviors that seem to characterize quality instruction. We have categorized these behaviors under the rubrics of presentation, practice, performance, and feedback, as shown in Figure 3. Although presented in a somewhat linear sequence in the figure, these behaviors usually occur in a cyclical fashion, with the sequence varying according to the lesson's content.

By presentation we mean the introduction and development of concepts and skills. The first behavior is an *overview* of the lesson. The teacher provides a *review* of previously learned concepts and skills, explains *what* is to be learned, and provides a reason for *why* the lesson is important (Bloom, 1976; Fisher et al., 1978; Good and Grouws, 1979).

The second behavior in the presentation portion of the lesson is

---

[2]See Huitt and Segars (1980) for a review of these instructional models.

Figure 3. Instructional Events Related to Quality Instruction.

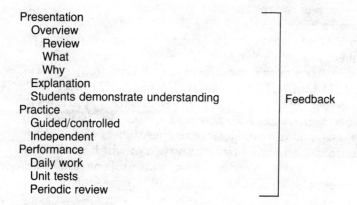

Presentation
  Overview
    Review
    What
    Why
  Explanation
  Students demonstrate understanding   Feedback
Practice
  Guided/controlled
  Independent
Performance
  Daily work
  Unit tests
  Periodic review

explanation, when the teacher develops or explains the concepts and skills to be learned. This explanation should be a planned part of the lesson (Fisher et al., 1978), focusing on the concepts and skills to be learned rather than on specific worksheet directions (Good and Grouws, 1979). Throughout the explanation, the students *demonstrate their initial understanding* of the concepts and skills to be learned, perhaps by responding to oral questions. The teacher continually provides *feedback* as to whether the students' understandings are correct, and if not, provides and explains the correct answers. This provision of feedback and correction is one of the key concepts underlying a "mastery learning" strategy (Bloom, 1976).

Studies by Fisher et al. (1978) and Good and Grouws (1979) emphasize the importance of providing a structured lesson and explaining concepts and skills fully and clearly. Also, these same studies recommend devoting more time to presentations for large groups and increasing the number of academic interactions between teacher and students. These interactions can be increased by asking students more questions (Fisher et al., 1978; Good and Grouws, 1979) and by establishing fast-paced instruction (Kounin, 1977).

After the teacher is satisfied that students have developed an initial understanding of the lesson, the students are ready to practice what they have learned. They begin under *guided or controlled* conditions by completing one or two short tasks under close supervision. Then they work *independently* with little or no teacher guidance. Several studies indicate that this independent practice should occupy from 25 to 50 percent of the allocated time for the subject area (Fisher et al., 1978; Good and Grouws, 1979).

Several teacher behaviors are related to improved student practice. For example, teachers need to give clear and specific directions about what to do (Fisher et al., 1978) and hold students accountable for completing their academic work within the required time (Anderson et al., 1979; Fisher et al., 1978; Good and Grouws, 1979). Again, teachers provide *feedback* about students' answers and explain once more if necessary.

Finally, student performance on *daily work*, on *unit tests*, and on *periodic review* is monitored. Students in effective classrooms spend at least half of their time working at a high level of success on daily work and less than 5 percent of their time working at a low level of success (Fisher et al., 1978). Students' mastery of a unit's content is evaluated every two to four weeks, with subsequent corrective feedback and remediation that lets all students master the content tested. Periodic review is provided on a regular basis (for example, weekly or monthly) to maintain mastery of concepts and skills (Good and Grouws, 1979).

Changes in instructional strategies do not have as dramatic an impact as do changes in management strategies. Nevertheless, teachers report making changes they believe do affect students' involvement and success. For example, a number of teachers use the list of instructional events shown in Figure 3 as a basis or checklist for their instructional planning. This has had an impact on the format of their instruction, especially the inclusion of reviewing the previous lesson and explaining the purpose of the lesson and why it is important. Teachers also report that they are more aware of students' responses and are providing correction with feedback, rather than simply stating that an answer is right or wrong. Most important, though, teachers report that they are continually assessing their instructional techniques and modifying those techniques when their students' behavior tells them that modification is needed.

Implications for Action

We have highlighted two sets of classroom characteristics that are related to student achievement, particularly in the basic skills. The relationship between student behaviors and student achievement is so strong that we can argue that, when students are involved, covering appropriate content, and successful on classroom tasks, there is a high probability that they will be achieving as well as or better than expected. In addition, we have described teacher behaviors relating to planning, managing, and instruction that can have an impact on student behavior. Now we would like to suggest why these characteristics are particularly useful as a focus in supervision, inservice, and other instructional improvement efforts.

First, as a result of recent research, most of the behaviors described above have been defined in such a way that they are readily observable (see Appendix 1 for suggestions for monitoring student behaviors). Because of their relationship to student achievement, observations of these behaviors can yield indicators of classroom effectiveness and help teachers, principals, and supervisors identify areas of strength and areas for possible improvement. Observations also can be used to assess "in real time" the effects of classroom improvement efforts.

Second, the student behaviors and their relationship to student achievement have a face validity for most educators and lay persons. Obviously, students will be apt to score poorly on achievement tests if they have not been taught the content covered by the tests in a way that enables them to achieve a high level of success on a day-to-day basis. It further follows that students will be more apt to achieve day-to-day success if (1) their lessons start from where the students are, and (2) the classroom is managed and the instruction is delivered in ways that are appropriate for their individual learning styles and that catch their attention and involve them.

Third, each of the student behaviors can be logically linked to other important aspects of the classroom and school. Thus information on any specific characteristic may be used to stimulate inquiry into a series of related areas. To be specific:

• If evidence suggests that student engaged time is relatively low, teachers and supervisors might examine:
  —allocated time for various instructional objectives
  —protection of allocated time from unnecessary disruptions
  —management strategies for controlling student behavior
  —how children are socialized to the norms of both the school and the classroom.

• If evidence suggests that students are not covering an adequate amount of criterion-relevant content, teachers and supervisors might examine:
  —teacher attention to students' prior learning
  —the content taught that is not criterion relevant
  —the match between the test content and the textbook content.

• If evidence suggests that students are not experiencing an adequate level of success, teachers and supervisors may need to reexamine all the areas relating to the design and implementation of instruction, including:
  —teacher attention to student characteristics and to the scope and sequence of learning tasks

—the modes of instruction used
—the quality of feedback provided students.

In conclusion, then, we believe recent research has identified at least three student behaviors that can be used as indicators of effective classrooms. Research has also identified a number of teacher behaviors that can be used to affect student behavior. The challenge now is to design and implement programs that encourage teachers, principals, and supervisors to take advantage of this knowledge.

We are aware, though, that when attending to these behaviors, attention must also be given to orchestrating and integrating them with the other factors making up the complex environment called a classroom. For example, research indicates that student learning is facilitated by an appropriate match between students' entering ability and the assignment of tasks. In a normal heterogeneous class, this means that ability grouping within the classroom might be necessary. However, other research indicates that students are more likely to be engaged if taught as a whole group. Therefore, a higher success rate for low-ability students may come at the expense of a lower engagement rate for the whole class.

In addition, teachers must be able to orchestrate and integrate their own behaviors. In fact, Hunter (1979) defines teaching as "the process of making and implementing decisions, before, during, and after instruction, to increase the probability of learning." We propose, then, that any inservice program must concentrate on two areas. First, teachers and supervisors must learn to attend to these important student behaviors on a day-to-day basis. Second, and equally important, teachers must develop the ability to make decisions regarding their appropriate selection and implementation of planning, management, and instruction strategies to increase involvement, coverage, and success. These professional skills can be developed through a positive supervisory process, which is the subject of the next chapter.

3.

Administering Effective

Classrooms: Conflicts in

Positive Supervision

Tom, a beginning third-grade teacher, is having problems with students doing seatwork during reading groups. He's spent time developing learning centers, but the students are still interrupting reading group instruction with questions. Tom and his principal, Bill, decide to explore the problem further during an upcoming observation. In the classroom, Bill records each student's engagement. This information helps Bill and Tom decide how to improve students' patterns of time use. As a result, Tom feels more successful and less threatened by the process of supervision.

Mary's standards for writing are not going to change, no matter how poorly her students perform. As a supervisor, Bill examines his own assumptions about student success and is able to confront conflicts in his supervisory beliefs while Mary changes her own professional practice.

In this chapter, Bill, Tom, and Mary use a supervisory process to improve their professional practice by focusing on the student behaviors of engagement and success—not without problems, however. Indeed, problems or conflicts are part of any supervisory experience. When supervisors and teachers understand that such conflicts are inherent in supervision, both will be able to improve their professional roles.

Supervision that supports classroom teachers' efforts to increase student involvement, success, and coverage may lead to increases in student achievement—if supervisors help teachers plan, manage, and instruct so that there is an increase in student involvement, success, and coverage of appropriate content. These six areas relate directly to student achievement, as the model introduced in Chapter 1 shows (see Figure 1). Every supervisor should be proficient in observing classrooms, conferencing, and planning with teachers to improve performance in these areas. Supervision that is practiced in this way *can* make a difference.

Past research has not concluded that supervision has much impact on student achievement, however, largely because the content of supervision in these studies was undefined. As recently as 1973, Cogan, a pioneer in the field, lamented, "The still unbridged gap between the observed behavior of teachers and the learning outcomes of students, represents a serious weakness in the use of observational systems in clinical supervision" (p. 160).

The problem has been confounded by the fact that many supervisors don't really supervise, but act instead as curriculum implementers. Some become the superintendent's assistants, and others lose their jobs in budget crises. Building principals have stepped into the breach, faithfully shouldering the burden of teacher supervision again. But for most administrative personnel, supervising classroom instruction consumes relatively little time (Ellet, Pool, and Hill, 1974). Conducting classroom supervision is relegated to the back burner while other fires are being put out.

Successful supervision is possible, however, given some important if's. It is possible *if* the superintendent places a priority on principals monitoring classrooms, *if* the principals internalize supervision as part of their professional role, *if* appropriate training is provided, *if* they know what to look for, and *if* they can manage the conflicts (Vann, 1979; Bailey and Morrill, 1980; Ryan and Hickcox, 1980; Neagley and Evans, 1980). Recognizing the discomfort and conflicts in supervision is a first step toward improving supervisory practice.

Supervision is an uncomfortable experience. It isn't like making friends, or working with a peer on a project. Unfortunately, textbook descriptions of warm, caring, and friendly educational supervision mask the conflicts inherent in the process. In reality, supervision calls up feelings of inadequacy, of being judged, of having to conform to the arbitrary standards of others. Supervisors as well as teachers feel conflicts and tensions within this relationship. Bad decisions, capri-

Figure 1. Supervision Supports Effective Classrooms.

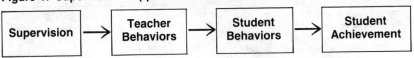

ciously made, affect personal and professional lives. Control is lost. A yearly evaluation elicits discomfort. These are natural feelings about the uncomfortable experience of supervision. For the moment, take two aspirins and read on.

The Domains of Supervision

Supervision in the helping professions usually consists of three roles: the supervisor (such as principal, content area specialist, or department chairperson),[1] the supervisee (in this case, the teacher), and the client (the student).

We define the supervisor as a person who has formal authority to evaluate or rate a professional's performance within an organization, or as someone who has input into such evaluations. It is the supervisor who has the major responsibility for communicating and refining the organization's intentions, such as improved student achievement, to those who are evaluated (Etzioni, 1964). The supervisor's role links the purpose and goals of an organization to the role of the supervisee (the teacher) and to improved services for the organization's clients (the students).

The teacher's role is to help students learn, which implies providing students with time to learn and appropriate content to learn in ways that promote student success.

The student or client helps the teacher and supervisor keep score. The supervisor and teacher use students' behaviors to determine whether the improvements planned have been successful.

In a positive supervisory experience, the goal is to improve the organization's capability to deliver valued outcomes (and student achievement is one we value) through the supervisor's and teacher's increased competence in performing their professional roles. Supervision, then, is centered on improving professional performance, although at times, the supervisor and supervisee may delve into more personal matters (Herrick, 1977; Squires, 1978, 1981). Cogan (1973) would argue that the domain of supervision should be limited strictly to teachers' behavior patterns, but this prohibition does not recognize the meanings professionals attach to their behavior. On the other hand, supervision is not a therapeutic or counseling relationship (Hansen,

---

[1]One could also see the superintendent of small and medium-sized districts serving this function with their principals. In this case, the teachers are seen as third party, while the superintendent serves in the role of supervisor and the principal in the role of supervisee. However, given certain minimum conditions, the supervisory relationships and processes would be the same.

1971). What appears to differentiate supervision from therapy is the emphasis on improving a professional role (Squires, 1978). Thus, the process of supervision consists of the supervisor and supervisee exploring the patterns of their behavior and interaction, and the meanings associated with those patterns.

Certain assumptions are implicit in this definition. First, we assume that professional behavior is observable and patterned. If one enters a classroom, one can observe all the activities going on there—students looking around the room and asking questions of other students, for example. Further, this observable behavior is patterned; that is, the behaviors show some consistency and regularity over time. For example, classes begin and end with some regularity. Some teachers begin the lesson when the bell rings; others begin after all students are seated at their desks. The instructional process itself is usually patterned as well. It consists of such segments as review, presentation of new material, guided practice, and independent practice. Not only are most classroom environments patterned, but people's interactions with their environment also form patterns. For example, Ms. Jones patterns her class so lessons begin on time, students keep busy, and homework is assigned after the bell has rung. Ms. Jones also knows that, despite this intentional patterning of the environment, if Mary sits by Tasha, neither will complete her seat work. Teachers and students live these patterns most of the time. The patterns help to reduce uncertainty and provide a safe and predictable environment in which to work and learn. Such behavior patterns may promote or discourage students' learning.

In our definition of supervision, we also assume that individuals attach different meanings or values to the same behavior patterns. They do so by relating the behavior patterns to different criteria, such as "professional manner," "student achievement," or "student self-concept." For example, two individuals may disagree on the appropriateness of a teacher-directed, structured approach to teaching because one values students' achievement on standardized tests while the other values students' learning to take charge of their own lives. Both may see the same quiet, task-oriented class, yet they would interpret the behavior patterns differently. Like these two individuals, most of us make mental leaps from the behavior we observe to inferences about that behavior. We have a tendency to judge what we see by personal standards and by our own beliefs about what is good, true, and right. While it is not possible to stop our leaps from data to judgment, in the professional world of teaching and supervising we must be able to explicitly trace the path of our judgments back to the data, and teachers and supervisors must share that journey throughout the supervisory experience. We must also be able to state explicitly the criteria that are being used to make judgments.

Student and teacher behavior patterns do significantly affect instructional outcomes, and for that reason they can form the foundation of the school's supervisory system (Bailey and Morrill, 1980). The key here is to have those behaviors take on meaning for teachers and instructional supervisors within the school. In the next section, we will discuss one format that can provide a structure for the supervisory relationship and thus reduce the conflict and tension associated with supervision.

A Format for Individual Supervision

Having an agreed-on format for individual supervision provides structure and safety for reducing conflicts in the supervisory relationship. In this section, we explain an individual supervisory format by describing the steps of a "clinical" supervisory cycle. Research documenting the effectiveness of this format is reported in Sullivan (1980). More detailed rationales and explanation of this format can be found in Cogan (1973), Goldhammer (1969), and Goldhammer, Anderson, and Krajewsky (1980).

The clinical supervisory models consist of at least four steps: (1) a preconference, (2) an observation, (3) analysis and reflection, and (4) a follow-up conference or postconference. It is generally assumed that the school has provided appropriate training for all staff in the format of the supervisory model and has a clear way of rating professional performance that is understood by the staff and is consistent with teacher association contracts.

The suggestions made in this section are prescriptive and are intended for administrators and teachers who are new to supervision. Naturally, both supervisor and teacher will adapt to their roles as supervision progresses.

The Preconference

During the preconference, the supervisor and teacher set the goals for the upcoming observation. These goals are consistent with both the general goals set by the supervisor and teacher during previous supervisory sessions and the goals of the organization. Specific data-collection methods are reviewed to determine if they are appropriate for the goals to be accomplished. A time is set for the observation, with the teacher's assurance that the time is appropriate for observation of the problem at hand.

When both supervisor and teacher have some common experience with the supervisory process, the preconference may last only five minutes. Supervisors and administrators just beginning this process in a schoolwide effort, on the other hand, will realize the value of fully modeling a preconference to provide the teacher with vital understandings necessary to the successful beginning of a positive supervisory experience. During the preconference, both supervisor and teacher establish an environment in which the ground rules are known.

The Observation

The purpose of the observation and the type of data to be collected are established during the preconference. The administrator or supervisor arrives at the classroom on time and takes his or her place in a location agreed on during the preconference. The supervisor does not interrupt either the teacher or the students during the lesson, unless such interruptions were agreed to in the preconference. During the observation, the supervisor records the data in the manner agreed on during the preconference. The supervisor may also note other data not included on the particular form being used but pertaining to the goals identified in the preconference.

Because students are generally the best source of evidence that learning is taking place, the supervisor is advised to spend time looking for and recording student patterns. Teachers appreciate this, as some patterns may go unrecognized by the teacher, especially in large classrooms. The supervisor resists the impulse to find fault with the teacher, noting instead the many positive behavior patterns that contribute to students' learning. The supervisor knows from experience that, in many of the school's classrooms, the majority of the learning-teaching patterns promote students' learning.

The supervisor realizes the importance of taking detailed notes on classroom patterns, as this provides a helpful history for the teacher and supervisor to use in discussing the class during the postconference. The supervisor also uses the notes to jot down hunches or hypotheses to discuss later with the teacher. When leaving, the supervisor remains as inconspicuous as possible. No judgment about the class is made at this point, for the patterns identified during the observation need to be discussed more fully with the teacher at the postconference. The supervisor leaves with a goodbye and a promise to meet with the teacher during the next few days. As both teacher and supervisor have been trained in data gathering and pattern analysis, the supervisor duplicates a copy of the observation notes and gives them to the teacher.

Analysis and Reflection

After the observation, the teacher may want to make notes on classroom patterns and areas for discussion during the postconference. After receiving the supervisor's notes and making an appointment for the conference, the teacher sets aside time to carefully reflect on both sets of notes and discern patterns that appear in the data. The supervisor also takes time to prepare for the conference by reviewing the observation form and jotting down a few areas that relate to the goals identified in the preconference. The supervisor further reflects on the positive patterns that assisted student learning, as these provide the key for helping the teacher improve in the identified goal areas. The supervisor may want to list several areas on which to focus during the conference.

Thus, both teacher and supervisor have studied, analyzed, and reflected on the data generated by the observation. Both have discerned patterns in that data. And both teacher and supervisor come to the conference with areas that they wish to discuss in relation to the goals set during the preconference. By completing these tasks beforehand, both the teacher and the supervisor help ensure that the postconference will be productive.

The Postconference

The postconference allows the teacher and the supervisor to share the meanings of the professional behavior patterns they have identified in order to improve their professional role performance. One postconference format is suggested in Figure 2. To keep the conference on track, beginning supervisors may want to keep a copy of this format on their desks and give a copy to the teacher. This is not the only conference format available, of course. See Acheson and Gall (1980) for other examples. Whatever conference format is agreed upon, both supervisor and teacher need to practice its use. Once both are proficient, variations will come more easily.

The Five Phases of a Supervisory Experience

The clinical supervisory cycle and the Champagne-Morgan conference strategy shown in Figure 2 provide a structure for reducing conflict over the short haul. In this section, the conflicts inherent in a long-term supervisory experience are described.

Just as the experiences of colleagues change over a lengthy relationship, so do those of supervisors and teachers. In fact, the total supervisory experience is made up of many supervisory cycles and many conferences. To feel at ease in a supervisory relationship, as uncomfortable as that relationship may be, it is helpful to recognize the five distinct phases of the supervisory experience and to be familiar with

Figure 2. The Champagne-Morgan Conference Strategy.[a]

Phase I: Setting Goals and Commitments to a Goal

Step 1. Objectives are specified/reviewed: *"We decided to take a look at two patterns in your teaching."*

Step 2. All data relating to objectives are shared: *"Let's talk for a few minutes about how you see this and how I see it given the data we already have, before we begin to suggest ways to deal with it."*

Step 3. Agreement is made to focus on "key" objectives: *"This seems to be the key issue that we can begin to work on today."*

Step 4. Agreement is made that some behavior changes are appropriate: *"Am I right that you want to try to do that differently?"*

Phase II: Generation and Selection of Procedures or Behavior

Step 5. Positive, appropriate behaviors in the setting related to the objectives are identified and reinforced: *"What was that neat thing you did today? Perhaps we can build the new procedure on that."*

Step 6. Alternative behaviors or reemphases are identified and examined: *"Before we decide what we are going to do, let's try to think of three or four different ways to approach this."*

Step 7. An alternative behavior is selected: *"Which one of these ideas do you think seems the best one to begin working with?"*

Step 8. Detailed implementation plans for the selected alternative are completed: *"Now that we've selected a way to go, our next step is to plan in detail what that means."*

Step 8a. (If appropriate) Plans made are practiced or role-played: *"Try out Steps 1 and 3 of this process on me here, now. We may need more work on it."*

Phase III. Commitments and Criteria of Success Are Specified

Step 9. Criteria for successful implementation of selected behavior are decided and agreed on: *"Will you suggest some ways we can measure or know whether our plans are working?"*

Step 10. Feedback is shared on purposes, commitments, and perceptions of the conference: *"We have worked on ____ today. What do you think we have accomplished?"*

Step 11. Commitments of both parties are reviewed: *"Okay, here is what I have promised to do, and here is what I think you have promised to do. Do you agree?"*

Conference Terminates.

[a]Champagne and Hogan (1978). Used with permission of the authors.

the specific conflicts that are attendant on each phase.

The five phases are (1) entrance, (2) diagnosis, (3) technical success, (4) personal and professional meaning, and (5) reintegration.[2] During the entrance phase, supervisors and teachers may experience conflict about the structure of supervision. The diagnosis phase may bring to light conflicts over the teacher's need to improve and the role of the

[2]The above phases were summarized from two studies of positive supervision, one from a supervisee's point of view (Herrick, 1977) and one from a supervisor's viewpoint (Squires, 1978, 1981). The results are generally consistent with findings of the investigators in the fields of counselor education (Kell and Mueller, 1966), social work (Pettes, 1967), psychiatry (Ekstein and Wallerstein, 1958), and teacher education (Goldhammer, 1969), and are similar to other typologies in the literature (Horgan, 1971; Gross, 1974; Schuster et al, 1972).

supervisor as helper. The technical success phase may produce conflicts stemming from an increasingly open relationship and from the additional demands success brings to both supervisor and teacher. During the fourth phase, both the supervisor and the teacher overcome conflicts about delving more deeply into the professional meanings and personal implications of their improving professional patterns. Reintegration, the fifth phase, occurs as the supervisor and teacher overcome conflicts about ending the supervisory relationship and integrating the improved professional patterns into their everyday habits.

The phases of a positive supervisory experience are different from the steps of a clinical supervision cycle. The clinical cycle consists of four steps that help to guide the supervisor's and teacher's interactions in the short term. The five phases of positive supervision occur over a more extended period of time. For example, a supervisor and teacher may complete a number of clinical supervisory cycles and still be working toward the technical success phase. Indeed, they may never go past that phase, even though they complete many clinical cycles.

Two stories—one from a teacher's perspective and one from a supervisor's—will serve as a base for describing the phases of positive supervision.

Tom's Story

In the first story, Tom, a beginning third-grade teacher, describes his experience with positive supervision focusing on one of the factors that affect student achievement: engagement. To set the scene, Tom met with the supervisor (in this case, Bill, the elementary principal) on two occasions. At the first meeting, Bill told Tom about the district's policy for supervising beginning teachers and specified how Tom would implement this policy. This discussion accomplished one of the tasks of the entrance phase. They talked about both participants' expectations for supervision and set up the first supervisory cycle. After the first cycle, Tom and the principal agreed it would be profitable to take a more in-depth look at the patterns of time use in the classroom. Here is Tom's description of the second clinical supervisory cycle, which took place in February of Tom's first year:

After the first supervisory cycle, Bill thought we might take a look at how students were using time in the classroom, and I agreed. Besides, Bill was the boss, and I was having trouble keeping the reading groups and the rest of the class busy at the same time. I'd work with one reading group and could never seem to have enough worksheets to keep all the other kids busy. Someone was always fooling around, and I'd have to stop the group and get the kids back to work. I had worked hard setting up activity centers in the class for kids to use after their worksheets, but these also caused some problems, because sometimes the directions weren't clear (it's hard to write directions for third graders) and so they'd come and ask me—again interrupting the reading group.

During the preconference, Bill and I talked about this problem. He began by commenting on what a lot of work I'd put into the centers and said that during his last observation, the centers appeared not to be working out as well as I had expected. Indeed that was true. I was relieved that Bill thought I was doing a good job.

He asked me to explain some of my goals and purposes for constructing the centers. Basically, I said I wanted to use them as an enrichment experience (perhaps the fancy term would impress him) after kids were through with their worksheets from the reading group. He told me that it looked like what I wanted to do was to keep the kids busy on a variety of reading activities. I agreed with that one too.

Bill explained that he would come in and be my "eyes" in the class during a reading period. He would record, once every two minutes, what each child in the classroom was doing according to the following scheme:

1. *Involved in reading group*
2. *Working on worksheet*
3. *Working in activity center area.*

I gave him the names of the kids in each of the three reading groups and the seating charts, and he said he would make an X on the chart by the kids who were paying attention or doing their work, and an O by the kids who weren't. He said he'd make a copy for me after the observation and we'd look for patterns in the data. Well, it sounded a little complicated, but I figured he knew what he was doing. Besides, it might be interesting to really know what the kids were doing while my back was to them during the reading groups. We set the time for the observation.

I knew he was coming, so I worked hard on making sure directions for the activities in the center were understandable. I even tried them out on a few kids before the observation day. When these children showed me that they understood the directions, I put their names on the bottom of the cards so that if the other kids had questions, they wouldn't have to interrupt me. Why didn't I think of that sooner?

Next, I made sure the worksheets were interesting and reinforced the skills I was teaching. I even prepped the class a little on what would happen when the principal came to visit. He would sit at the side of the room and take notes, and the students were to pretend he was just a desk or a chair. The kids thought that was pretty funny.

And that's what happened. I wasn't bothered by his taking notes; I knew what he was taking notes on. After a few minutes things settled into a routine. I was a little nervous, but my extra preparations helped me feel more confident. And the kids seemed to want to "look good for the principal." I really had a heightened sense of what I was doing, especially those little slips I made. But then I remembered that Bill was looking at the students and not at me. After observing, he smiled and left.

I was curious about what he had found out. After school I picked up the filled-in observation sheets and took a look at them. It was complicated. At the bottom of the sheets were some notes: "Total engagement rate for class, 70 percent; engagement rate for reading groups, 90 percent; engagement rate for kids working on worksheets, 50 percent; engagement rate for students in centers, 60 percent."

We had decided to meet during one of my planning periods the next day for the postconference. I had jotted down some notes about the observation sheets, but I was curious and a little suspicious about the numbers. What did they mean? Would I be rated on just the numbers? I decided to wait and see, but I would also have my defenses ready for using just numbers to determine my rating.

When I came into Bill's office, we got right to the task at hand. It almost seemed too abrupt. Bill did most of the talking at first. He reviewed with me how he had recorded the data and determined all the engagement rates. I was fascinated by all that information about just one small aspect of teaching. Bill briefly reviewed a little of the research and gave me copies of some articles to read. He talked about the standard 75- to 85-percent engagement rate and said that I had come pretty close. He complimented me on the attention I received from the kids in the reading groups and said I would soon have the rest of the class working just as well. He also praised the fast-paced discussion and my ability to pull all the kids in for comments. He said they really seemed to be listening to each other. Then he asked how this activity was different from working on seat work or at the centers. "Perhaps once we review the differences, we can incorporate more of what is working in your reading groups in the other activities," Bill said. "That would probably help to improve engagement rate in those two groups." We came up with the following list of differences:

Reading Group	*Other Groups*
Teacher-directed	Self-directed
Interactive	No interaction with others on the task at hand
External pacing by teacher	
Everyone "knew" they were going to participate	No opportunity for interaction
	Everyone working independently
	No clear way of giving rewards to those who did the work in the way expected

I had never really thought about the different groups in that way. From the list, there doesn't appear to be any reason why there couldn't be only two groups *in the classroom instead of three. That would mean less time for students working alone. And there didn't seem to be any reason why kids had to work alone at the centers, or even wait for me to check their worksheets, except that was the way I set it up.*

I mentioned these ideas to Bill, who said they were great and that I should try some different arrangements and see how they worked. He offered only one piece of advice—that I should face the room while conducting the reading group. "Very often," he said, "just a look at a misbehaving kid is all that's necessary."

The conference time was getting short. Bill asked me to try a few of these ideas and let him know how they turned out. He offered to return to the class when the changes I was going to try were going smoothly. If I needed any assistance, his door was always open before and after school, or by appointment during my preparation period. I left the office with a few minutes left before the next class.

I was excited about the new understandings I had about my classroom. I was also surprised that we had come up with just a few ideas but nothing really specific. I will check with the other third-grade teacher about some of my ideas to see if she has any suggestions. I am beginning to trust Bill a little more. He seemed to know the right questions to ask, yet wasn't dogmatic about the answers. He gave me enough rope, but I don't feel out on a limb alone.

From experiences such as this, we have synthesized the five phases of a positive supervisory experience as one way of charting the inherent conflicts of supervision and their resolution. Tom's story provides a framework for discussing the first three phases.

Entrance

In each phase, the supervisor and teacher are confronted with a number of tasks. For example, in the entrance phase, they must establish a structure for the supervisory process, which may resemble the preconference, observation, analysis and reflection, and postconference format suggested earlier. This task has the potential for blocking or stopping the supervisory relationship because of personal and professional conflicts. For example, in the entrance phase, the teacher who agrees to a particular supervisory format is submitting to the supervisor's judgment. This may foster in the teacher feelings of professional and personal inadequacy, which must be overcome if a positive supervisory experience is to occur. On the other hand, the supervisor also experiences the conflict of knowing that a structure is necessary but not wanting to impose constraints on the teacher.

Both supervisor and supervisee can block progress during any of the phases by not adequately resolving the professional or personal conflicts inherent in the supervisory tasks. Blockage can also result from not accepting the tasks of supervision or trying to shortcut them. For example, Bill and Tom both agreed that the activity centers would be the focus of the supervision, thus allowing the process to continue. Because the task was clear and Bill and Tom agreed on it, there was no blockage.

By adopting a four-step clinical cycle of supervision, Bill and Tom completed the major task of the entrance phase—agreeing on a structure for supervision. The school district and teachers associations play important roles in the entrance phase, as they prescribe how supervision and evaluation will be structured for most employees of the district. When there is no structure in place, supervision may be difficult because there is no consensus on the supervisory format or structure. Conflicts will then surface around the supervisor's and teachers' attempts to set up a structure for supervision, and possibilities for a positive supervisory experience will likely be blocked.

When Tom accepted the supervisory cycle, he also accepted the legitimacy of Bill, the principal, as a person who conducts supervision. As Tom said, "Bill was the boss." While Bill's reactions aren't related in this story, he might also be experiencing tension from conflicts inherent in being a supervisor. He may question his own adequacy as a supervisor, even though he has been successful before. He knows that a new supervisory relationship means putting himself on the line; having to be cautious, yet open; hoping for good results, but knowing all the things that can go wrong.

Tom probably feels more at ease during the second cycle than the first, and the initial anxiety for both Tom and Bill is relieved somewhat as they create a relaxed atmosphere in which Tom's expectations can be discussed. Bill also indicates to Tom that he affirms Tom's intentions and capabilities. Tom states, "I was relieved that Bill thought I was doing a good job."

Diagnosis

The task of the diagnosis phase is to reach agreement on problems, strategies, and solutions for improving professional behavior. Bill started out on a positive note by discussing the work Tom had put into the activity centers. This provided continuity from the last supervisory cycle, and the centers had been on Tom's mind as he prepared for the preconference. Agreement was needed on the problems to be addressed during supervision.

The danger in the diagnosis phase is that the teacher will accept the supervisor's definition of the problem or that the supervisor will describe a problem that may not be appropriate or important for the teacher. Tom's reaction to the observation plan reveals a little of this conflict: "Well, it sounded a little complicated, but I figured he knew what he was doing." Bill took a chance in defining the plan without Tom fully understanding the meaning of the data. As Tom put it, "I was curious and a little suspicious about the numbers." Nevertheless, there appeared to be sufficient trust in the relationship that Tom's suspicion did not block further progress.

It is during the diagnosis phase that data is usually collected, and that task may also create conflicts. Collecting data validates a problem if one exists, and validating a problem may be perceived as dangerous, breeding resistance and blockage. Tom says, "I would also have my defenses ready for using just numbers to determine my rating." The supervisor may use such resistance to diagnose problems between the supervisor and the teacher. In fact, Bill begins the postconference by explaining the data-collection method to Tom, thus addressing indirectly Tom's unstated conflict about the use of data. At other times, such resistance may be discussed directly between supervisor and teacher.

The supervisor's initial focus in the diagnosis phase is on the teacher's interaction with students. Thus Bill suggests a continuing focus on activity centers. Bill also shows respect for Tom's authority and integrity by listening to his diagnosis of the problem without making judgments about his actions. The supervisor may experience the problem of making judgments about the teacher's situation but still indicating acceptance of the teacher. Bill handles this conflict by explicitly stating his judgment—that the centers were not working out as well as Tom had expected—in a way that confirms Tom's intuition. Bill also states the goal—keeping students involved in reading—while reinforcing Tom's efforts in that direction. This strategy overcomes potential conflicts, as Tom had prepared well for the observation.

Technical Success

During the third phase, the supervisor and teacher experience success by improving instructional patterns. The supervisor initiates active interventions in areas where the teacher needs assistance and is ready to learn. Bill's intervention is to propose generating a list of the differences between the learning centers and teacher-directed instruction. Because Bill and Tom had successfully completed the tasks of the entrance and diagnosis phases, success was more likely here. Bill was able to meet Tom's need for a rather loose structuring of the situation without giving in to any feelings he might have had about making sure all areas of improvement were covered. Thus, the supervisor must consider the teacher's ability to learn and change successfully without imposing the supervisor's own time schedule. This may be tricky, as some teachers block progress through delay or by always acquiescing to the supervisor's wishes. In this case, Bill felt Tom was not resisting and would follow through because of his commitment to improving the centers.

Technical success focuses on improving students' learning, and the supervisory experience should be judged mainly on those terms. We assume that Tom's changes in the classroom will increase student engagement in academic activities. With such a focus, supervision avoids conflicts about who is right or wrong, and who won or lost.

The supervisor's relationship with the teacher is a model that is often copied by teachers in their relationships with students. In this case, we might assume that Bill's strategy of letting Tom decide how to implement ideas generated during the conference will transfer into Tom's allowing more flexibility in students' use of the learning centers. Tom states, "There didn't seem to be any reason why kids had to work alone at the centers, or even wait for me to check their worksheets." Bill has allowed control to be vested in Tom, just as Tom is allowing more control over the learning process to be vested in his students.

Technical success is supported in an environment in which mistakes can be made without fear of failure, and feelings can be explored without questioning the worth of individuals. The relationship focuses on future improvements, rather than on detailed analysis of past mistakes. Bill, for example, suggests that Tom try a few of the ideas and report how they turn out, allowing Tom to deal with the problems in ways he deems appropriate. Tom can accept or reject those ideas on the basis of his own criteria. Bill makes available professional knowledge—such as suggesting that Tom face the class while working in small groups—without dominating the discussion. The supervisory experience deepens as success builds trust and confidence. Tom recalls, "I am beginning to trust Bill a little more. . . . He gave me enough rope, but I don't feel out on a limb alone."

Bill's Story

In the next story, Bill, the principal, reports on his experience while supervising Mary, a tenth-grade English teacher with three years of experience. Bill describes part of a clinical supervisory cycle concerning a conflict between Mary's standards for her students' writing and her encouraging their success—an important area for improving students' achievement. Bill examines his own patterns of behavior and thought in his professional and personal life and begins to change the way he interacts. Such a change indicates he is in the fourth phase of positive supervisory experience, examining personal and professional meanings for himself. Later he integrates these learnings and his professional life returns to "normal"—thus describing the fifth phase of positive supervision, reintegration.

Our preconference ended with Mary stating quite adamantly that her standards for writing were not going to change. We had agreed, during the ten-minute preconference, to take a look at students in her tenth-grade class who were successful in meeting those writing standards. The observation would be held in three days' time, when students would be working in groups correcting their writing assignments. The classroom observation was only one part of our data collection effort. We were also collecting folders of student compositions to take an in-depth look at students' progress in writing during the past six months, a project initiated by the English faculty. And we also used Mary's grade book.

We had known each other professionally for three years and had successfully completed a number of supervisory cycles. Her classes were pleasant, orderly, and task oriented, and she was able to convey a real feeling for the beauty of the English language to her students in ways that they could understand. At times, her classes were slightly mechanical, but no one would question her competence and dedication. In light of our previous experience, then, her adamant reaction about maintaining standards appeared incongruous to me.

The students were not fulfilling Mary's expectations in written composition. There may have been a number of reasons, including Mary's instruction, the meanings she gave to the idea of standards, or the amount of time the students were spending on the activities. Perhaps there is an inherent conflict between helping students succeed and also requiring that they be graded according to whether they attain a certain standard. Schools, after all, sort students (pass and fail) as well as assist in their learning. Those are two hats that are difficult to wear, as I know from my previous role as vice-principal for discipline. The same feelings came across that I felt when I first took the "disciplinarian" job: "We must have clear rules. We must enforce them. Otherwise, the school will go out of control. It will be my fault for not enforcing the rules." The same kind of tension may be at work in Mary's classroom.

During the classroom observation, Mary reviewed the writing standards from an overhead transparency and then divided the kids into pairs to correct each other's papers. This appeared to be a frequently used proofreading routine. I went around the room to the students identified at the preconference to see what they were doing and talk with them. I also reviewed their folders. Mary went where students asked for help. I made a note on the seating chart Mary had given me of who Mary helped, and I made brief notes on what was in the cumulative writing folders.

Let me summarize some of the patterns I noticed in Mary's class—I'm sure there were also others—then backtrack to some of my own feelings and reactions and the meanings I attached to those patterns. (1) There did not appear to be any purpose for pairing the students. For example, two students who both had spelling problems were paired together, and they had a difficult time catching each other's mistakes. (2) There was no explanation required of or given by *students to each other about their mistakes. (3) Neither the class nor individuals appeared to be moving toward any specific goals. (4) From data in the folders of the successful students, all appeared to be meeting the standards, but they appeared to have had this ability from their first composition. (5) From the students I talked to, about 60 percent of the students in the class felt the idea of standards was an imposition on them. It was an onerous task, and they didn't see the point. Well, while some of that is just griping, there seemed to be genuine confusion in the students' minds about the purpose of the writing standards. (6) Mary's own explanation to students was, "You'll need this for college or to get a job." It was odd that Mary should still be supplying a rationale to gain commitment to these writing standards when they had been the focus of class attention for some time.*

On leaving the class, I understood a little more about Mary's frustration with the writing standards. However, I surmised that the standards weren't the salient issue at all. The fact was, these tenth-grade students weren't cooperating and, indeed, weren't learning and succeeding. Neither was Mary. Mary's frustration stemmed from the students' resistance to learning—at least that was my hunch. She may see the students' actions as a rejection of what she is trying to teach, perhaps even a rejection of herself as a teacher. Her adamant posture in the preconference may be another indicator of her feelings of frustration.

Perhaps there is a cycle here. Her students aren't succeeding; she feels frustrated that she isn't succeeding; she keeps trying, though less and less. Thus, class activity descends into ritual. Perhaps I should mention this in the postconference. The six patterns I identified would support doing so.

I played out such a conference scenario in my mind. I felt depressed. Mary has probably tried to get out of this cycle and failed. Bringing it up would reinforce the failure. I mean, why can't she see what is happening? I feel frustrated and angry with her in my own imaginary scenario, in the same way I suspect that she feels frustrated with her students.

It's at this point that something clicks—my own patterns of reaction become clear to me. I am looking for frustration rather than success, because that is what Mary directed my attention toward. In the scenario, I have reinforced that through the patterns I observed in the classroom. I was not conscious or aware that Mary's definition of the problem was becoming my own. I needed to recognize this in order to be able to break my own pattern, and to break the cycle of frustration for myself with this new understanding.

I had fooled myself into thinking I was looking for success: the observation of students who were succeeding, the gaps I identified in the instruction of students not being paired with a purpose, the emphasis on Mary's justification of the standards. Yes, they were all patterns, but all patterns that reinforced the students' lack of achievement and Mary's frustration.

I decided those were not the patterns to share in the follow-up conference. Instead, I thought back to the observation to look for patterns that did show success. There were the writing standards and Mary's concern about them. The students did have folders for a cumulative record of their writing. The students did go through the motions of correcting each other's papers, certainly saving the teacher much time. Some students had mastered the standards—a potential resource. The standards were written down and shared with the students. It was beginning to fit together in my head. Now, the problem was how to get Mary to see and use the potential of these positive patterns during the conference.

Even months later, I am still reflecting on this incident, particularly my own reactions. While supervising Mary, I had allowed her way of looking at the situation to become my own. Her frustration was transferred to me, so that I saw frustration in our supervisory relationship. In a sense, I let her use me to confirm her own meanings until I began to recognize the pattern and did something to break out. I had to break the pattern before she could. I guess what a supervisor does is to "see beyond." Luckily, Mary was able to break the frustration cycle.

In interacting with other teachers, I am now aware that they might try to transfer their frustration to me, and I need to ask if the reality they define is one that allows for professional growth and for their own success. I need to understand the teacher but not lose myself, not let go of my own perspective.

While thinking about these dynamics, I also realized that I might transfer my own frustration and insecurities to the teacher. Focusing on those six classroom patterns would have been a sure way to keep Mary frustrated in her teaching of writing. In fact, by highlighting and emphasizing those patterns, I may have created my own problems. Mary is, after all, a sensitive person and a very hard worker.

The success I finally experienced with Mary during this particular supervisory cycle is overshadowed by what I am learning about my own interaction patterns and the dynamics of the supervisory process. Indeed, I almost can't help but extend thoughts about professional behavior into my personal life. For example, what expectations do I project for my own wife and children? Do we construct our worlds in ways that allow us options for success? How do I promote or take back options in my own interactions? Not that I think about this all the time, but such thoughts do occur to me.

Mary made a similar comment the other day. "I don't know whether you realize this, but when you shared with me your own reactions to my frustration in teaching writing, it made a lot of sense to me. I think what may have happened was that I was feeling a lot of frustrations with my six-year-old at the time—he just won't listen—and perhaps a bit of that frustration spilled over into my class and my teaching." She didn't go into much more detail, and I really didn't feel comfortable knowing too much more. However, those kinds of comments are rewarding because they let me know I'm on the right track.

Mary has become less dogmatic with her students, and I feel I haven't been as rigid with the teachers I supervise. My relationship with Mary is easier, too. There isn't as much tension—perhaps because we were able to successfully deal *with the writing standards and all they symbolized, both for her and for me. I know we both learned from our experience. The positive approach to supervision has taken on new meaning for me.*

Personal and Professional Meaning

From reports like these, we have synthesized some ideas that appear in most positive supervisory experiences during the fourth phase—examining meaning for self—and the fifth phase—reintegration.

During the fourth phase of a positive supervisory experience, the focus of the interaction shifts from concentration on the teacher's interaction with students, to examination of the personal meanings evolving from the teachers' or the supervisor's improving professional practice. Thus Bill has shifted his concentration from assisting Mary with her teaching to examining his own patterns of interaction with her.

In examining the meanings of improved professional practice, the teacher or supervisor may reveal personal conflicts and uncertainties, as well as personal history, expanding the range of content that is acceptable between teacher and supervisor. Both may become aware of how specific feelings, beliefs, and attitudes can interfere with or facilitate interactions with the others in the professional setting. For example, when Bill played out the scenario of the postconference, he felt depressed. Rather than go ahead with the conference anyway, Bill used this feeling as a basis for examining his own reactions. By using this approach to reduce his internal conflict, Bill experienced a change in professional skill, knowledge, and self-perception. He recognized the influence Mary was having on his patterns of interaction with her, then generalized that to interactions with future supervisees.

Personal and professional growth for both supervisor and supervisee evolve from this shift to a more personal level, and the supervisor-supervisee relationship is deepened. For example, even after a couple of months Bill still values what he learned while considering Mary's postconference. This shift to a personal level also affects Mary. As Bill explains, the relationship is easier, and there isn't as much tension. Mary is able to share with Bill her source of frustration, and Bill considers Mary's increased technical competence a validation of their success.

In a positive supervisory experience, the supervisor is aware of this shift and explores personal meanings to improve professional performance. Personal concerns are not necessarily resolved, however. Although the content of the supervisory sessions has expanded, the supervisor controls the depth of involvement, thus maintaining the objectivity necessary to reflect on further changes in a professional manner. For example, Bill shares with Mary the processes he has used in deciding how to structure the postconference, but he does not share these interaction patterns with his own wife. Neither does he inquire further about Mary's six-year-old. Again, the supervisory experience is aimed at promoting professional, not personal, growth. Personal growth should be only a secondary outcome of a positive supervisory experience.

In this phase, the supervisor examines the changing nature of his or her role with the teacher, feeling both more freedom and more caution in the relationship. The supervisor is gratified by the increasing technical competence of the teacher and thus feels that the format and content of supervision can be less structured. For the supervisor, there is a heightened sensitivity to the teacher, and the relationship deepens as a result.

Reintegration

During the fifth and final stage, both supervisor and teacher consolidate the knowledge, the increased professional performance, the heightened self-awareness, and the self-examination of the earlier phases into their professional repertoires and personal lives. The fourth stage's constructive tension of dealing with professional concerns through personal conflicts is now reduced. Satisfaction is communicated.

Bill has become more aware of his own patterns when dealing with a teacher's frustration. By looking at these patterns on both a personal and a professional level, Bill has learned more about himself and the process of supervision.

Summary

A positive supervisory experience happens when a supervisor and a teacher can overcome the conflicts that are inherent in each phase of the supervisory experience. These conflicts are summarized in Figure 3.

To recapitulate briefly, during the entrance phase, the supervisor must provide enough structure to get started without dampening his or her relationship with the teacher. The teacher, on the other hand, wants to improve but must submit to judgment in order to do so. During diagnosis, conflict centers on the issues of disclosure, judgment, and trust. The technical success phase is characterized by conflicts in overcoming procedural difficulties. During the personal and professional meaning stage, conflicts arise over efforts to maintain a balance between personal and professional issues. Finally, during the reintegration phase, conflict centers on reducing the supervisor's and teacher's dependence on each other, which develops naturally as part of any positive supervisory relationship.

Supervisors and teachers who can successfully address involvement, success, and coverage and resolve the conflicts inherent in the supervisory process are likely to improve student achievement as well. What's more, they are likely to view the entire experience as a positive

Figure 3. Examples of Conflicts in Supervisory Experiences.

Phases of Supervision	Teacher's Conflicts	Supervisor's Conflicts
Entrance Example of a Task: A structure for supervision (in other words, clinical supervision is discussed)	Being judged vs. knowing one could improve	Establishing appropriate formats and structures so that the teacher feels comfortable, while maintaining avenues for future growth
Diagnosis Example of a Task: The focus of supervision is decided upon; an agreement to work on that focus is made	Fear of disclosure of personal and professional inadequacies vs. professional concerns, trusting the supervisor	Sensing teacher's conflicts/problems while not making judgments
Technical Success Example of a Task: Supervisor and teacher experience success on the focus of supervision	Justifying the status quo vs. accepting, trying, and overcoming difficulties	Resisting imposing a "personal" schedule on the teacher, while ensuring that success (in the teacher's terms) happens, and encouraging teacher's continued growth
Personal and Professional Meaning Example of a Task: Supervisor and teacher examine what implications the success has for their professional roles and personal lives	Disclosure to the supervisor of the more personal meanings of technical success	Controlling depth of involvement with teacher's more personal concerns while maintaining balance with professional change
Reintegration Example of a Task: Consolidation of meanings for professional and personal self, integration of technical success into professional repertoire, and disengagement from supervisory relationship	Feeling comfortable in using newly acquired skills and understanding while resolving conflicts about dependence on the supervisor	Letting go in a successful relationship while wanting to continue in this powerful stage

one that will enhance the effectiveness of the classroom and the school. The result for both supervisor and teacher is increased technical competence in performing a professional role.

Learning and growth are evident in the supervisor, the teacher, and the student. The feedback from students continues to be positive, and problems move toward a solution. The teacher has become aware of how specific feelings, beliefs, attitudes, and behaviors can interfere with or facilitate interactions with students. The teacher has also come to assess changes in his or her behavior in terms of their impact on the students, rather than in terms of winning the supervisor's approval. The teacher experiences competence, self-confidence, and trust in his or her professional judgment. The teacher and supervisor have explored and come to a fuller understanding of personal conflicts that affect the performance of a professional role. Both are more open and less dogmatic. This expanded conception of the self by the teacher or supervisor has been integrated into the professional practice of each. The supervisor's positive experience validates and reinforces his or her philosophy and approach to supervision. The supervisor generally becomes more trusting and open to the supervisory relationship and process. The teacher-supervisor relationship has come to resemble that of colleagues. Both teacher and supervisor have become more autonomous.

4.

Effective Schools:

What Research Says

Pick a school you know and ask these questions about its climate:

- Does the school have an orderly environment?
- Does the school promote an academic emphasis?
- Are there expectations for success?

Then ask three more questions about its leadership:

- Are models of appropriate behavior, attitudes, and beliefs encouraged by the school's climate?
- Has a consensus developed around patterns of acceptable behavior and around the academic emphasis of the school?
- Does feedback to school participants provide a large number of rewards distributed over most of the population, as well as punishments that are consistent?

These questions have been synthesized from the research literature on effective schools (Squires, 1980). The school's climate and leadership are necessary ingredients in supporting the teacher behaviors of planning, classroom management, and instruction that, in turn, foster student success, involvement, and coverage of appropriate content. As the model in Chapter 1 shows, improved student achievement is the likely outcome.

Three areas appear important in creating a positive school climate: an academic emphasis, an orderly environment, and expectations for success. Three leadership processes that build and maintain this climate are modeling, consensus building, and feedback. These, at least, are our conclusions after reviewing the research on effective schools (Squires, Huitt, and Segars, 1981).

46

Different types of studies are included in this review: (1) studies that concentrate on quantifiable input-output relationships, (2) studies that look at the correlates of safe schools, (3) studies that compare high- and low-achieving schools, (4) a longitudinal study of urban schools succeeding above expectations, (5) studies of successfully desegregated schools, and (6) descriptions by journalists of schools with reputations for effectiveness. The studies were chosen because they used a wide variety of methodologies, were relatively well known and accessible, and attempted to associate a wide variety of variables with schooling outcomes. While the review covers a large number of studies, it is not intended to be comprehensive.

We have chosen to summarize the results by turning the conclusions into questions that teachers, administrators, superintendents, and school board members can ask to determine the effectiveness of a school. For example:

Finding	Question
Student reports of strict enforcement of school rules and strict control of classroom behavior are associated with low levels of school property loss (NIE Safe School Study, 1978).	Do students perceive congruence among the faculty in enforcing school rules and strictly controlling classroom behavior?

In the following chapter, we group the questions to illustrate how the themes of school climate and leadership emerged for us.

We would like to stress that the results reported here are based either on correlational studies or on descriptive case studies, and it is therefore risky to infer causation. Still, the consistency across studies using various methodologies is strong enough for this line of research to merit a closer look, particularly as it provides a potential body of knowledge for those who make school policy and desire school improvement.

Our discussion is organized around input, process, and outcome. Examples of these terms include the following:

Input: students' socioeconomic status; students' IQ; school size

Process: courses are planned jointly by teachers; high proportion of students hold leadership positions; administration checks that teachers assign homework

Outcome: standardized test scores; student behavior; attendance, delinquency, violence, and vandalism.

We begin by summarizing studies that ask, "What inputs generally affect a school's outcomes?" Then we review research suggesting that a school's processes are related to its outcomes. In the third part of the chapter, we summarize a longitudinal study that confirms this relationship between processes and outcomes. Next, studies of effective desegregated schools are summarized. Finally, journalists' descriptions of effective schools test some conclusions of the more rigorous research. Throughout, we highlight questions derived from the research to stimulate thought on characteristics of effective schools. Then, in Chapter 5, we cluster these questions into groups and discuss their implications.

The Search for Input-Output Relationships

During the 1950s and 60s, educational research focused on relationships between a school system's inputs and outcomes. These studies were generally on a large scale and tended to concentrate on areas that could be easily quantified. (Averch, 1974, reviews a substantial amount of this research. Bridge, Judd, and Moock, 1979, and Sweeney, 1982, review research done more recently.)

The input conditions in these studies generally included such factors as the number of books in the library, amount of leader experience and/or college preparation of school staff, availability of instructional materials, dollars spent on instruction and administration, and socioeconomic level of students. On the output side were such things as grades, entrance into college, dropout rates, Scholastic Aptitude Test scores, and achievement test results. If research found a significant association between input measures (such as dollars spent on instruction) and outcomes (such as student grades or college acceptance rates), the results could become the basis for recommending that more money or more emphasis be placed on those aspects of schooling.

James Coleman (1966) conducted perhaps the best-known study in this area. With the exception of socioeconomic status (SES), which did tend to show a high correlation with pupil performance, Coleman found no significant relationship between the inputs and outcomes he examined: "Only a small part of variation in achievement is due to school factors. More variation is associated with the individual's background than with any other measure" (p. 7). The input conditions of a school's physical plant, its services, its extracurricular activities, and the characteristics of teachers and principals did not appear to be associated with student achievement.

There are three common interpretations of Coleman's findings:

1. Despite all the resources put into schools, they are not able to

affect student achievement. Therefore, schools should receive fewer resources.

2. If SES is what makes a difference, then putting more resources into schools serving poor students is likely to affect their achievement. (Title I/Chapter I legislation resulted from this line of thinking.)

3. With the exception of SES, what was studied did not appear to make much difference. Therefore, other aspects of schools should be examined.

By now the furor and debate has subsided, and most educators and researchers have embraced the third option. The search now focuses on other school characteristics.

We would like to add a footnote to this brief review of the Coleman Report, however. Coleman also found that, in addition to SES, student attitudes showed the strongest relationship to achievement. Student attitudes were divided into three components: interest in learning and reading, self-concept, and environmental control. Of these three components, Coleman concluded that "the child's sense of control of environment is most strongly related to achievement" (p. 320). Thus, students who feel that luck is more important than hard work, and that something or somebody is stopping them when they try to get ahead, are less likely to succeed in school than are those who believe otherwise. Two questions arise from these findings:

● Do students believe that luck is more important than hard work?
● Do students believe that they can get ahead without something or someone stopping them?

The Search for Process-Outcome Relationships

The Coleman Report indicates that the most easily measured characteristics of school context, with the exceptions of SES and student attitude, are not associated with student outcomes. This suggests that something in the school environment influences those attitudes. The review of studies in this section attempts to track down those influences.

Processes That Lead to an Orderly Environment

The studies in *Violent Schools—Safe Schools: The Safe School Study Report to the Congress* (1978) sought process factors associated with school violence and vandalism and a safe and orderly environment. Our review here links school effectiveness with low amounts of violence and vandalism.

From a random sample of urban, suburban, and rural schools across the United States, 15 factors were associated with the extent of crime in a given school. The authors organized these factors into five closely related themes and concluded that, "taken together, they suggest a set of overall process goals that schools should work to achieve" (p. 132). These themes provide the basis for our questions, which, when answered, point the way to effective schools. Most of the themes involve a school's processes, rather than community influence or socioeconomic factors. The study's findings are shown, according to our paradigm, in Figure 1.

One theme arising from these factors is that the size and impersonality of a school are related to school crime:

Large schools have greater property loss through burglary, theft, and vandalism; they also have slightly more violence.

The more students each teacher teaches, the greater the amount of school violence.

The less students value teachers' opinions of them, the greater the property loss (p. 132).

In larger schools, especially when classes themselves are also large, it is more likely that students can "slip through the cracks" and go unnoticed. In addition, in an impersonal school where there is little contact between teachers and students, students are less likely to be affected by teachers' opinions. We will return to the effect of teachers' opinions and expectations later; for now, one question arises:

• Do teachers have extensive contact with a limited number of students in several aspects of their education?

Three factors suggested the Safe School Study's second theme—systematic school discipline:

Student reports of strict enforcement of school rules and strict control of classroom behavior are associated with low levels of school property loss.

Student perceptions of tight classroom control, strictly enforced rules, and

Figure 1. Findings of the 1978 Safe School Study.

Input	Process	Outcome
Rural	Size and impersonality	Violence
Suburban	Systematic school discipline	Vandalism
Urban	Arbitrariness and student frustration	
	Reward structure	
	Alienation	

principal's firmness are associated with low levels of student violence.

Reports by the teachers of strong coordination between faculty and administration are associated with a lower level of property loss (p. 133).

Perceptions of coordinated discipline and tight classroom control may indicate that there is enough social interaction among school participants for a consistent disciplinary policy to be developed and carried out. Also, students are likely to perceive this consistency in the principal's firmness and teachers' tight classroom control. These findings suggest the following questions:

• Has the principal built shared expectations and strong coordination about school rules?

• Do students perceive congruence among the faculty in enforcing school rules and strictly controlling classroom behavior?

The third theme—arbitrariness and student frustration—suggests that student crime results when students perceive rules to be arbitrarily enforced by an unnecessarily punitive staff. As the study points out:

Schools where students complain that discipline is unfairly administered have higher rates of violence.

Schools where teachers express authoritarian and punitive attitudes about students have greater amounts of property loss (p. 134).

These two factors tend to exist in schools that have a weak or lax disciplinary policy. Such a policy may make students feel unfairly singled out for punishment, which, in turn, tends to increase crime. Because they see students as unruly, teachers begin to develop unfavorable attitudes toward them. The cycle of frustration escalates and ends up in violence and property loss. This suggests the following questions:

• Do students perceive that discipline is unfairly administered?

• Does the faculty express punitive or authoritarian attitudes toward students?

The fourth theme emphasizes the importance of a school's reward structure. Four factors appear related to violence and property loss:

Schools where students express a strong desire to succeed by getting good grades have less violence.

Schools where students express a strong desire to succeed by getting good grades have more property loss.

Schools where students have a strong desire to be school leaders have greater property losses.

Schools where teachers say they lower students' grades as a disciplinary measure have greater property losses (p. 135).

The last three factors indicate that an emphasis on getting good grades decreases violence but increases vandalism. The study describes this syndrome as "a situation in which the competition for rewards is intense, the availability of rewards is limited and the unfair distribution of rewards is prevalent. These students care about the rewards of the school but see the rewards being unfairly distributed; they react by attacking the school" (p. 135). This raises the following question:

• Are rewards earned fairly by a large number of students?

Rewards here can go beyond the academic rewards of grades. For example, being on a football team or in the band provides explicit recognition of special talent and a possible reward for that talent.

The fifth theme, alienation, appears to encompass many of the other themes that went before. The study defines alienation as "the breakdown of the social bond that ties each individual to society" (p. 136). One of the study's major findings touches on this concept directly:

Student violence is higher in schools where more students say that they cannot influence what will happen to them—that their future is dependent upon the actions of others or on luck, rather than on their own efforts (p. 136).

As we reported previously, Coleman also found that a sense of efficacy, of having control over one's destiny in the world, was strongly related to academic achievement. We believe that this sense of being connected to the larger society (and for children this means being a "part" of a school) is the most significant finding of these large-scale studies.

The importance of this finding is, in a sense, unexpected, considering the thousands of variables that were studied. Nevertheless, its implications for the school as a social institution appear to signal a need to weave students, faculty, and administration together into the fabric of the school and to let personal interactions demonstrate to students their ability to affect the environment. The following two questions emerge:

• Do students, faculty, administration, and the community feel that their own efforts govern their future?

• Does the social structure of the school teach those who live there that their actions have some effect?

Processes That Lead to Improved Student Achievement

The second group of studies in this section examines school processes while controlling SES variables in order to discover which of those processes are associated with higher student achievement. Researchers first aggregated outcome data by schools, then grouped the schools into categories according to students' SES, and finally examined processes in high- and low-achieving schools within SES categories that may account for achievement differences. The research concentrated on school-level variables. This strategy may be summarized as follows:

Input: control SES
Process: what processes make the difference?
Outcome: high-achieving or low-achieving school?

Interestingly, a number of these studies were conducted at the state's own initiative—in Maryland, New York, Michigan, Delaware, Pennsylvania, and California, for instance.

The findings did show differences among schools with students from the same SES levels. The following passage from Bookover et al. (1979) gives some results of these comparisons between high- and low-achieving schools:

Our data indicate that high achieving schools are most likely to be characterized by the students' feeling that they have control, or mastery of their academic work and the school system is not stacked against them. This is expressed in their feelings that what they do may make a difference in their success and that teachers care about their academic performance. Teachers and principals in higher achieving schools express the belief that students can master their academic work, and that they expect them to do so, and they are committed to seeing that their students learn to read, and to do mathematics, and other academic work. These teacher and principal expectations are expressed in such a way that the students perceive that they are expected to learn and the school academic norms are recognized as setting a standard of high achievement. These norms and the teachers' commitment are expressed in the instructional activities which absorb most of the school day. There is little differentiation among students or the instructional programs provided for them. Teachers consistently reward students for their demonstrated achievement in the academic subjects and do not indiscriminately reward students for responding regardless of the correctness of their response.

In contrast, the schools that are achieving at lower levels are characterized by the students' feelings of futility in regard to their academic performance. This futility is expressed in their belief that the system functions in such a way that they cannot achieve, that teachers are not committed to their high achievement, and that other students will make fun of them if they actually try to achieve. These feelings of futility are associated with lower teacher evaluations of their ability and low expectations on the part of teachers and principals. The norms of achievement as perceived by the students and the teachers are low. Since little is expected and teachers and principals believe that students are not likely to learn at a high level, they devote less time to instructional activity, write off a large proportion of students as unable to learn, differentiate extensively among them, and are likely to praise students for poor achievement (p. 143–144).

Our questions, taken from Brookover's description, ask those who are concerned with effective schools to look at how the schools reinforce positive expectations:

- Do students master their academic work?
- Do students feel the school helps them to master their academic work?
- Do principals and teachers believe and expect that students can master their academic work?
- Do teachers and principals support the academic focus of the school by spending most of the school day on instructional activities?
- Do teachers provide rewards for actual achievement?
- Is there little differentiation among students or in the instructional program provided for them?

In Brookover's descriptions there is a shift in perspective from the material aspects of the school—dollars spent, years of training, curriculum materials—to a cluster of attitudes and perceptions. For example, students believe that what they do will make a difference; teachers and principals expect students to succeed; the role of the principal emerges, as it did in the Safe School Study, as an important factor in effective schools.

In summarizing studies of high- and low-achieving schools, Austin (1979) found the principal's role to be important in supporting the belief systems held by teachers and students:

Strong principal leadership (for example, schools "being run for a purpose rather than running from force of habit").

Strong principal participation in the classroom instructional program and in actual teachings.

Principals felt they had more control over the functioning of the school, the curriculum, and program staff (p. 13).

Wellish et al. (1978) found that administrators in schools where achievement was improving were more concerned with instruction, communicated their views about instruction, took responsibility for decisions relating to instruction, coordinated instructional programs through regularly discussing and reviewing teaching performance, and emphasized academic standards.

Weber (1971), in examining four inner-city schools that were successful in teaching children to read, found eight factors that affected reading achievement: strong leadership, high expectations, good atmosphere, strong emphasis on reading, additional reading personnel, use of plans, individualization, and careful evaluation of student progress. All of these factors are usually under the direct control of the principal.

Certainly, there are other studies that support the need for strong leadership: Edmonds (1978), Felsenthal (1978), Irvine (1979), and McLaughlin and Marsh (1978) are a few. In addition, the Safe School Study also reported that:

the data point to the principal and the school administration as the key element. An effective principal who has developed a systematic policy of discipline helps each individual teacher to maintain discipline by providing a reliable system of support, appropriate inservice training for teachers, and opportunities for teachers to coordinate their actions (p. 137).

A number of questions emerge from these findings:

- Does the principal have a purpose in mind when running the school?
- Does the principal emphasize academic standards?
- Does the principal provide a reliable system of support, appropriate inservice training for staff, and opportunities for staff to coordinate their actions in the areas of instruction and discipline?
- Does the principal regularly observe classrooms and confer with teachers on instructional matters?

A Longitudinal Study

The next study, *Fifteen Thousand Hours,* by Rutter et al. (1979), is more sophisticated than the previous ones reviewed in that it tracked the performance of 12 inner-city London schools over a period of five years. The study controlled for SES and examined four outcomes: achievement, attendance, student behavior, and delinquency. Again, it concluded that school processes—the characteristics of a school as a social organization—influence the school's effectiveness. The study's components are categorized according to our paradigm in Figure 2.

Rutter and his colleagues suggest that the formation and maintenance of a social group, with norms and values that support the purpose of the school, may be the most important resource a school possesses. In addition, they suggest ways in which classrooms and teachers affect a

Figure 2. Components of Rutter's Study, *Fifteen Thousand Hours.*

Input	Process	Outcome
Control for SES	Academic emphasis	Achievement
	Skills of teachers	Attendance
	Teachers' actions in lessons	Student behavior
	Rewards and punishments	Delinquency
	Pupil conditions	
	Responsibility and participation	
	Staff organization	

school's climate. Because this study is powerful in its implications and conceptually elegant in its design, we have chosen to discuss its conclusions in more depth.

All 12 schools that Rutter studied had relatively similar students (input variables), but produced very different outcomes in terms of (1) academic attainment on exams, (2) student behavior in school, (3) attendance, and (4) delinquency.

For example, controlling for parents' occupation and students' verbal reasoning ability (two variables correlated with delinquency), Rutter found that for comparable groups of boys who happened to attend different schools, those in one school were three times as likely to be delinquent as were those in another school. Indeed, delinquency rates for boys varied from a low of 16 percent in one school up to 40 percent in another. The significant difference in these groups of students appeared to be simply that they attended different schools.

Upon finding that schools differed in outcomes, Rutter hypothesized that certain school processes influenced these differences and, further, that those processes were, for the most part, under the control of teachers and administrators. (Note how far we've come from the Coleman findings reviewed above.) For our purposes, Rutter's general findings can be summarized as follows:

1. Variations were partially related to student intake; namely, where there was a substantial nucleus of children of at least average intellectual ability, students generally scored higher on the tests. Delinquency rates were higher in those schools with a heavy preponderance of the least able. However, the differences in intake, while affecting outcomes, did not affect school processes.

2. The variations between schools were stable for five years and were not related to physical factors.

3. Better-than-average schools tended to perform at higher levels on all outcome measures.

The differences between the schools were systematically related to their characteristics as social institutions. These characteristics, the most significant of which are listed below, can be modified by teachers and administrators:

- Academic emphasis
- Skills of teachers
- Teachers' actions in lessons
- Rewards and punishments
- Pupil conditions
- Responsibility and participation
- Staff organization.

Measurement of these seven characteristics of effective schools provides further insight into what Rutter means by school processes. In Figure 3, each measure that is significantly associated with one or more outcome area has been changed to a question. As you review the chart, try out the questions on a school you know.

But this is not the end of the story, for Rutter also introduced the

Figure 3. Processes and Measures Associated with School Outcomes.

School Processes	Measures
Academic Emphasis	Is homework frequently assigned?
	Do administrators check that teachers assign homework?
	Do teachers expect students to pass national exams?
	Is work displayed on classroom walls?
	Is a large proportion of the school week devoted to teaching?
	Do a large proportion of students report library use?
	Is course planning done by groups of teachers?
Skills of Teachers	Do teachers spend a large proportion of their instruction with students involved?
	Do inexperienced teachers consult with experienced teachers about classroom management?
Teachers' Actions in Lessons	Do teachers spend a large proportion of time on the lesson topic?
	Do teachers spend less time with equipment, discipline, and handing out papers?
	Do most teachers interact with the class as a whole?
	Do teachers provide time for periods of quiet work?
	Do teachers end lessons on time?
Rewards and Punishments	
Punishment	Are there generally recognized and accepted standards of discipline uniformly enforced by leaders?
Rewards	Do teachers praise students' work in class?
	Is there public praise of pupils at assemblies?
	Is students' work displayed on walls?

School Processes	Measures
Pupil Conditions	Is there access to telephone and provisions for hot drinks? Is care in decoration of the classroom evident? Is there provision for school outings? Do students approach staff members about personal problems? Do teachers see students at any time?
Responsibility and Participation	Do a large proportion of students hold leadership positions? Do students participate in assemblies? Do students participate in charities organized by the school? Do students bring books and pencils to class?
Staff Organization	Do teachers plan courses together? Do teachers report adequate clerical help? Does the principal check to see that teachers give homework? Is administration aware of staff punctuality? Do teachers feel their views are represented in decision making?

concept of "ethos" or "climate"—the style and quality of school life—which he attributed to the norms and values of the school as a social organization. In explaining the concept of ethos, Rutter took a second look at the measures that correlate with outcomes and reorganized them into four areas: (1) group management in the classroom, (2) school values and norms of behavior, (3) consistency of school values, and (4) pupil acceptance of norms. We will discuss each category and then offer a series of questions based on Rutter's analysis.

Group Management in the Classroom

Rutter's findings about group management in the classroom are included here for two reasons. First, this study examines significant aspects of both the classroom and the school as a whole, and Rutter contends that the social structure of a classroom in an effective school reinforces and supports the norms and values—the climate—of the whole school. Second, the Rutter study reinforces the importance of students' engagement and success and of teachers' planning and managing instruction.

Rutter found that children's classroom behavior was much better when the teacher had prepared the lesson in advance, when the teacher arrived on time, when little time was wasted at the beginning in setting up, and when the teacher mainly directed his or her attention to the class as a whole. These findings suggest a structured classroom in which lessons begin and end on time and students' attention to the lesson is high. Our questions, then, are:

- Do teachers plan lessons in advance?
- Do teachers start lessons on time and continue without interruption?
- Is whole-group instruction used?

School Values and Norms of Behavior

Rutter suggests that values and norms are communicated and reinforced through three social mechanisms: (1) teachers' expectations about children's work and behavior; (2) models provided by teachers' conduct and by the behavior of other pupils; and (3) feedback children receive on what is acceptable performance at school. We will discuss each of these mechanisms in order.

Teachers' expectations and standards. The Brookover et al. (1979) study touched on teacher expectations as a potent indicator of effective schools. Rutter suggests that these expectations can be communicated to students by regularly assigning and marking homework, giving students responsibility for bringing books and pencils to class, and providing students with numerous opportunities to exercise leadership. Questions arising from these findings are:

- Do teachers expect students to succeed?
- Do teachers regularly give and mark homework?
- Do students bring books and pencils to class?
- Does the social structure of the school and classroom provide opportunities for students to practice leadership?

Models provided by teachers. Standards of behavior as modeled by the school's staff also reinforce a school's climate. Positive models convey the message that the school is valued because staff members attempt to keep it clean and attractively decorated, to begin lessons on time, to be sensitive to the needs of children, and to give their own time to assist students. Negative models show that teachers do not value the school, do not start classes on time, do not spend class time on the lesson, and do not discipline students in ways sanctioned by the school. Two questions arise from these findings:

- Are positive models of behavior provided by teachers?
- Does teacher behavior, such as helping students on the teacher's own time, indicate that the school's children and the profession of teaching are valued?

Feedback. Feedback to students can also support the norms, values, and climate of the school. According to Rutter, "Feedback that a child receives about what is and what is not acceptable at school will constitute a powerful influence on his behavior" (p. 189). Rutter found that praise during lessons happened on the average of three or four times a lesson; surprisingly, there were three times as many negative reinforcers. The amount of punishment showed only weak, insignificant associations with outcome, however, while the amount of rewards and praise, particularly during lessons, was associated with better student behavior. Rutter cautions that when giving praise, the currency should be real; the children should have actually performed in a commendable fashion. As we have seen in Brookover et al. (1979), students' success is important not only for its probable effect on self-concept but also to support the norms and values of the school. More rewards than punishments, then, may be another indication that the social and task structure of the school promotes student success. Rutter also points out that when punishments are necessary, they should be given in a way that indicates firm disapproval without humiliating the student or modeling violence. Questions for assessing schools according to these findings are:

• Does the feedback students receive in terms of rewards or praise outnumber the punishments?

• Do teachers praise students for work well done?

• Do teachers structure the classroom environment to permit students to succeed?

• Are punishments delivered in a way that indicates firm disapproval of misbehavior while avoiding humiliation and avoiding modeling violence?

Consistency of School Values

Rutter describes a school's social organization by the degree of consensus held across the school's population: "The 'atmosphere' of any particular school will be greatly influenced by the degree to which it functions as a coherent whole, with agreed upon ways of doing things which are consistent throughout the school and which have the general support of all the staff" (p. 192).

For example, Rutter found better student outcomes in schools where teachers planned courses jointly; where expectations for behavior and discipline were set by the staff as a group; where administrators were aware of staff punctuality and homework assignments; and where decisions were centralized and staff members perceived that their interests were represented in those decisions. Rutter's suggestion that a school's staff take its cues from administrative behavior and values reinforces studies that suggest the principal's role is to help set the norms and values of an institution. Together, the staff and the administration appear to be most influential in developing and maintaining a school's climate through consensus and consistency of norms and values.

For those who want to confirm a school's effectiveness, the following questions may be appropriate:

• Have teachers and administrators come to a working consensus on patterns of acceptable behavior for staff, students, and administration?

• Does there appear to be a working consensus on how school life is organized?

• Are there structured opportunities for staff and administration to develop and reinforce consensus?

• Do teachers feel their interests are represented by those making decisions?

Pupil Acceptance of School Norms

Students must accept the school's norms if the school is to be effective. Rutter suggests three crucial influences in determining this acceptance. The first, general conditions for pupils and staff attitudes toward pupils, leads to the following questions:

• Is the building maintained and decorated to provide pleasant working conditions for students?

• Are staff members willing and available for consultation by children about problems?

• Does the staff expect students to succeed and achieve?

Shared activities between staff and pupils, such as away-from-school outings, also contributed to better student outcomes. Rutter hypothesizes that these shared activities may increase effectiveness if they are directed toward a common goal or purpose, such as a schoolwide charity. A question that reflects this point is:

• Are there out-of-class activities that bring students and teachers together to build toward a common goal?

Pupil behavior and success on exams were also influenced positively when a high proportion of students held positions of responsibility. Rutter hypothesizes that students who hold positions of responsibility are more likely to identify with the educational values of the school and to provide models of mature behavior for others. The following question might be posed:

• Do high proportions of students hold positions of responsibility?

To summarize, the Rutter study shows that differences in school outcomes in such areas as academics, attendance, student behavior, and delinquency not only reflect a school's intake patterns but are, to a significant degree, determined by school processes and characteristics.

Studies of Effective Desegregated Schools

Delving into the research literature on desegregation, we found similar school processes operating in effectively desegregated schools. These processes are outlined in Figure 4. (See Henderson, et al., 1981, for a concise review.)

From a student's point of view, equal access and participation in the academic and cocurricular activities of the school was an important dimension associated with successful desegregation. Thus, rigid tracking tends to teach children that only a few will succeed (Pettigrew, 1975; Crain, 1978; Jones, et al., 1972; Porwoll, 1978). Similarly, equal and fair access to social positions and cocurricular activities are important (Rist, 1978, 1979; Schofield, 1978). Even school symbols, like team colors and mascots, can be a powerful force in fostering a sense of ownership by all groups in a school. The following question might be posed:

• Do students have equal and fair access to academic and cocurricular school programs?

Codes of conduct are important in a successfully desegregated school, as they are in a safe school. Studies point to a need for a uniform code of conduct, firm discipline, and procedures that are perceived to be fair by all groups (Lincoln, 1976; Migell, 1978; Wilie and Greenblatt, 1980). The principal appears to be the key person in establishing the "working" code of conduct and the climate of the school. The successful principal is able to communicate expectations of fair play to all staff and students (Egerton, 1977; Noblit, 1979). A question reflecting this is:

Figure 4. School Processes and Outcomes in Desegregated Schools.

Input	Process	Outcome
Schools under study as desegregated institutions	Student participation Codes of conduct	Reduction of conflict
	Principal's leadership Faculty models and expectations Inservice training	Successful desegregated schools Improved achievement

• Is the principal perceived by students and faculty as modeling expectations of fair and equal treatment?

High expectations are also important, for what children learn depends to a large degree on what teachers expect of them (Davey, 1973; Eddy, 1976; Mackler, 1969). Moreover, a desegregated faculty may help provide positive role models for children (Cohen, 1980; Davidson, 1978). Two questions arise:

• Do school personnel provide positive role models for children?
• Do teachers have high expectations for all students, regardless of race or class?

Inservice training is one way a school demonstrates commitment toward the goal of equal opportunity. Successfully desegregated schools provide staff with inservice on skills for teaching heterogeneous classrooms and skills in classroom management, as well as self-analysis in actions that indicate discriminatory behavior. A question that comes from this discussion is:

• Is inservice training provided that encourages self-reflection and skill building in areas promoting equal opportunity?

Descriptive Studies of Effective Schools

Recent research findings on effective schools have been indirectly confirmed in a rather unusual way by a group of journalists on a research fellowship at George Washington University's Institute for Educational Leadership. Their reports are compiled in D. Brundage, ed., *The Journalism Research Fellows Report: What Makes an Effective School?* (1979). After an overview of current research, the journalists were asked to visit schools across the country that local communities thought were effective or that had higher achievement test scores than would be expected. While journalistic descriptions do not hold the validity and reliability of research data, we think they ring true enough, and are consistent enough with the research, that useful questions can be posed from them. For the most part, our reading of the *Journalism Research Fellows Report* parallels that of Robert Benjamin of the *Cincinnati Post*, who wrote one of the articles. Benjamin found that effective schools are similar in terms of their principals, beliefs, instruction, teachers, reading, and resources. We will describe all but reading and resources because our own analysis of the *Journalism Research Fellows Report* doesn't support these as major characteristics of effective elementary and secondary schools.

Throughout the articles, the principal emerged as the one who sets focus, tone, philosophy, and direction in a school: "Good principals tend to rock the boat. They forsake the desire to be loved for the hard task of monitoring students' progress. They set achievement goals for their students, and they judge their teachers and themselves by them" (p. 102). Furthermore, the principals who were featured in this report tended to observe classes frequently, to have at least a partial say in hiring teachers, to actively structure the development of curriculum and instruction, to obtain the staff's commitment to a schoolwide program, and to elicit respect from students as a "straight shooter." Although the articles described both elementary and secondary principals with varying leadership styles, one of the headlines from the report summed it up: "Principals demand—and get—results, but allow flexibility in achieving them" (p. 24).

"Belief that students can learn—that the job can be done" (p. 102) is the second indication of effective schools. It appears from the news articles' descriptions that this belief originates with the principal and spreads to staff and students. But belief, from our analysis of the articles, goes beyond believing that children can and will learn. Belief also has to do with school focus, philosophy, and goals. The focus of a school could be a particular curriculum program, or an emphasis on community participation, or a successfully desegregated school. But there has to be a focus—a belief. As one of the headlines put it, "Good Schools Have Quality Principles."

"Instruction" is the third characteristic of an effective school. As Benjamin reports, "Student achievement results from time spent directly and efficiently on teaching academic skills" (p. 102). Task focus, a sense of urgency, and a belief that time is valuable all characterize effective classrooms. These classrooms appeared to be more humane places than classrooms where there was a lot of off-task behavior. Figure 5, based on logs compiled over two months of observation, shows that more time is spent on instruction in what Benjamin called "schools that work."

"Teachers" is the fourth theme mentioned in the articles, and in effective schools most teachers believe that children can succeed and have confidence in the principal's ability to lead. The effective teachers these reporters observed were able to maintain discipline in their classes without spending time punishing students, and the students appeared to understand the rules. Effective teachers planned their lessons in advance. When a teacher needed assistance, appropriate help was available from the principal or from another teacher. Effective teachers expected their students to learn and were able to structure their classrooms, using whole-group teaching techniques, to fulfill their

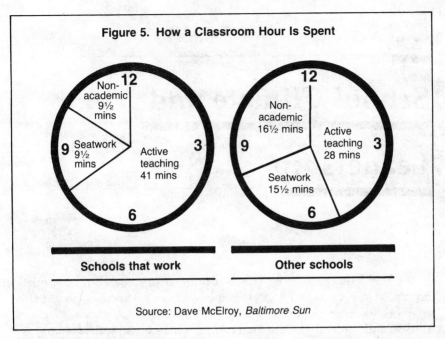

Figure 5. How a Classroom Hour Is Spent

Non-academic 9½ mins
Seatwork 9½ mins
Active teaching 41 mins

Schools that work

Non-academic 16½ mins
Active teaching 28 mins
Seatwork 15½ mins

Other schools

Source: Dave McElroy, *Baltimore Sun*

expectations. In effective schools, teachers handled most discipline problems themselves and rarely sent children to the principal's office. Furthermore, they cared for the students, had a sense of pride in teaching, and were relatively satisfied with teaching in a particular school. Effective schools usually did not have a transient teaching staff. The reporters did not paint rosy pictures of all the "effective schools," however; some still had problems with discipline (although most reported improvement), apathy, lack of student motivation, poor community relations, and large and insensitive bureaucracies. Nevertheless, these schools appeared to be moving in a set direction.

These journalistic descriptions of effective schools reinforce the importance of student engagement, student success, teacher management of instruction, and supervision by the principal, and as such they bolster the previously reported research on classroom effectiveness. Moreover, they suggest the following questions about effective schools:

● Does the principal actively set the tone and focus of the school by observing classrooms, enforcing the discipline code in a "fair but firm" manner, and setting goals for the school that are supported by the staff?

● Does the school have a focus or philosophy, a direction that is supported by administration, staff, and students?

● Is time spent efficiently and directly on teaching academic skills?

● Do teachers usually handle their discipline problems themselves?

5.

School Climate and

Leadership

In the previous chapter, we posed a number of research-related questions that can be asked to determine a school's effectiveness. In this chapter, we regroup those questions under the categories of school climate and leadership—the final components in our model for improving school and classroom effectiveness (see page 4.)

We recognize that others may group these questions differently, and we encourage you to take a stab at such an exercise. Our purpose is not to determine the critical categories of school effectiveness for all time; rather, it is to be as explicit as possible about the way the data make the most sense for us now.

School Climate

Metaphorically, school climate consists of three weather conditions: an emphasis on academics, an orderly environment, and expectations for success. The questions synthesized from the research provide indicators that can help assess a school's climatic conditions. Because all school participants appear to contribute to and have a stake in a positive school climate, the questions are grouped to indicate each participant's contributions to each "weather condition."

Academic Emphasis: Students

- Do students master the academic work?
- Do students bring books and pencils to class?

• Do students use the library on a weekly basis?
• Do students perceive congruence among the faculty in enforcing school rules and strictly controlling classroom behavior?

Students' mastery of academic work can be determined by report card grades, by questions correct on unit tests, and by the teacher's professional judgment. Not surprisingly, students who bring books and pencils to class usually succeed. Such actions by students reinforce the school's academic emphasis. Frequent use of the school library by students may indicate that students and teachers value the resources of the library, and are thus reinforcing an academic emphasis. The questions also suggest that when students perceive congruence among the faculty in enforcing school rules and controlling classroom behavior, the academic emphasis of the school is enhanced.

Academic Emphasis: Teachers

Instruction

• Is time spent efficiently and directly on teaching academic skills?
• Do lessons start on time and continue without interruptions?
• Is whole-group instruction used?
• Do teachers provide rewards for actual achievement?
• Do teachers praise students for work well done?
• Do teachers regularly give and mark homework?

Planning

• Do teachers plan lessons in advance?
• Do teachers regularly give and mark homework?

Other

• Do teachers expect students to succeed?
• Are staff members willing and available for consultation by children about problems?

Teachers can reinforce an academic emphasis by spending time efficiently and directly on teaching academic skills. This may help student engagement and success, which, according to our model, may in turn enhance student achievement. Planning lessons in advance helps to ensure that lessons begin and end on time. Teachers can bolster an academic emphasis by providing rewards and praise to students for work well done. Homework assignments also appear to be an indicator of academic emphasis. Homework gives a student an opportunity for further practice, thus increasing the student's engagement and increasing the likelihood of improved achievement. The availability of teachers to help students with problems may also signal an academic emphasis.

Academic Emphasis: Principals

Behaviors

- Do teachers and principals support the academic focus of the school by spending most of the school day on instructional activities?
- Does the principal regularly observe classrooms and confer with teachers on instructional matters?
- Does the principal check to see that teachers assign homework?

Structures

- Is course planning done by teacher groups rather than by isolated individuals?
- Do teachers feel their interests are represented by those making decisions?
- Are rewards fairly earned by a large number of students?

Beliefs

- Do principals and teachers believe and expect that students can master their academic work?
- Does the social structure of the school teach those who work and learn there that their actions have some effect?

Principals promote the school's academic emphasis by their own actions, by the organizational structures they put into place, and by their beliefs. Principals of effective schools tend to spend a large proportion of their day on activities related to instruction. Three actions are associated with high student achievement: checking that teachers assign homework, observing in classrooms, and conferring with teachers. Effective principals have found ways to organize their time so that the instructional program receives priority.

The questions also suggest that principals create organizational structures that enhance the school's academic emphasis—for example, having groups of teachers rather than individuals plan courses. In effective schools, teachers feel their interests are represented when decisions are made, although they may not have direct input into the decision. This finding suggests that adequate communication exists in the school. The question of students earning rewards implies that the school organizes reward structures for achieving students, and that achievement is a valued outcome. Principals of effective schools organize and maintain such reward structures.

The research on effective schools highlights the importance of principals believing that students will master the academic content. When the principal actively structures the school's social system around mastery, then it may be more likely that students and teachers feel their actions and efforts have some effect.

Orderly Environment: Students

Perceptions of discipline

- Do students perceive that discipline is unfairly administered?
- Do students perceive congruence among the faculty in enforcing school rules and strictly controlling classroom behavior?

Student participation

- Do students use the library on a weekly basis?
- Do students take care of school resources?
- Have students participated in organizing a schoolwide charity drive?
- Are a high percentage of students named in school assemblies for their participation?
- Do high proportions of students hold positions of responsibility?
- Do students have equal and fair access to academic and cocurricular school programs?

Students, teachers, and principals also contribute to a school's orderly environment, the second component of a positive school climate. The questions concerning this component suggest indicators of effective schools that have a low incidence of violence and vandalism and/or higher-than-expected student achievement.

Student indicators of an orderly environment can be grouped into two clusters: perceptions of discipline procedures, and participation in school affairs. In effective schools, students perceive that discipline procedures are fair and are applied equally to all. Effective schools also elicit high student participation: students take care of school resources, contribute to school-organized charity drives, use the school library, and are involved in class activities and assemblies. These specific indicators correlate with positive pupil behavior in school.

We go beyond these indicators to suggest that schools that enlist students' participation in a wide variety of activities are less likely to have student behavior problems because the students have a stake in the school. If many students interact around school activities outside the classroom, then norms of positive student behavior may be more likely to emerge.

Orderly Environment: Teachers

Instruction

- Do teachers start lessons on time and continue without interruption?
- Do teachers regularly give and mark homework?
- Do teachers provide rewards for actual achievement?

Classroom management

- Are positive models of behavior provided by teachers?
- Does the feedback students receive in terms of rewards and praise outnumber punishments?
- Are punishments delivered in a way that indicates firm disapproval of misbehavior while avoiding humiliation and avoiding modeling violence?
- Does the faculty express punitive or authoritarian attitudes toward students?
- Do teachers usually handle their infrequent discipline problems themselves?
- Are teachers available to consult with students about problems?

Teachers can enhance the orderly environment of a school through their skills in instruction and classroom management. In instruction, the teacher's use of time is important; thus one question suggests that teachers who maximize their allocated time by beginning lessons promptly have fewer discipline problems. Teachers who give homework and provide rewards or reinforcement for actual achievement also have fewer discipline problems. As these comments suggest, some indicators of orderly environment also reinforce a school's academic emphasis.

The classroom management questions suggest ways discipline problems should be handled in the classroom. For example, the teacher's own behavior is a model for student behavior. In classrooms with few behavior problems, teachers use punishment but avoid humiliation and violence toward students. Moreover, they do not express punitive or authoritarian attitudes toward students, and they tend to handle discipline problems themselves. Positive rewards and praise generally outnumber negative reinforcements. Teachers with fewer discipline problems also tend to be more available to students to talk about personal and academic problems. It is interesting to note that the two teacher behaviors of instruction and classroom management, which are closely linked to student achievement in our model, also promote an orderly school environment.

Orderly Environment: The Principal

Consensus building for an orderly environment

- Have teachers and administrators come to a working consensus on the patterns of acceptable behavior for staff, students, and administration?
- Has the principal built shared expectations and strong coordination about school rules?

● Does the principal provide a reliable system of support, appropriate inservice training, and opportunities for staff to coordinate their actions in areas of instruction and discipline?

Delivery of discipline

● Does the principal actively set the tone and focus of the school by observing classrooms, enforcing the discipline code in a "firm but fair" manner, and setting goals for the school that are supported by the staff?

● Are punishments delivered in a way that indicates firm disapproval of misbehavior while avoiding humiliation and avoiding modeling violence?

● Do students perceive that discipline is fairly administered?

The principal's role in creating an orderly environment revolves around creating a consensus about the school rules among staff and students, then administering this consensus in a "fair but firm" manner. In delivering punishment, firm disapproval should be indicated while avoiding humiliation and modeling violence. Students may be the "touchstone" if they perceive that discipline is fairly administered. Thus, consensus building and firm delivery help define the principal's role in creating an orderly school environment.

Expectations for Success

Students

● Do students feel the school helps them to master academic work?

● Do students believe that luck is more important than hard work?

● Do students believe that they can get ahead without something or someone stopping them?

Teachers and principals

● Do students, faculty, administration, and community feel that their own efforts govern their futures?

● Does the social structure of the school teach those who work and learn there that their actions have some effect?

● Do principals and teachers believe and expect that students can master their academic work?

● Do teachers expect students to succeed?

● Do staff expect students to succeed and achieve?

● Do teachers have high expectations of all students, regardless of race or class?

Expectations for success help reinforce an orderly environment and an academic emphasis in schools. But such expectations cannot be directly observed in behavioral terms. Indeed, this area is usually assessed by questionnaires that ask students, "Do you believe luck is more important than hard work?" and ask teachers, "Do you think that all of your students will complete high school?" In effective schools, positive answers to these questions generally coincide with teachers starting classes on time or principals observing classes. We assume that there is some interaction between beliefs and behaviors, but we are not sure whether people act because they believe, or act first and belief follows. We suspect it's a little of both.

Students in effective schools perceive that the school helps them master academic work. The teacher's behavior in structuring the classroom, and the principal's leadership in organizing the school, apparently help mold students' perceptions in this way. Such speculation is consistent with research on achievement motivation, which suggests that students can learn to suceed, given the appropriate structure.

We also speculate that academic success leads to enhanced self-concept and a feeling of efficacy on the student's part. Students in effective schools generally believe they can get ahead and that work is more important than luck. Self-concept is correlated with student achievement, and both are significant and measurable outcomes of schooling for us.

Teachers and principals in effective schools express their expectations for success in such a way that students know what is expected of them and believe they can measure up to these high standards. As a social system, the school also communicates its expectations for students by providing rewards for work well done and creating opportunities for student participation and leadership. In their attention to academic programs and discipline procedures, principals set the tone for the school. And in an effective school, both principal and teachers not only believe students can succeed, but model those expectations to the school as a whole.

School Leadership

When reviewing the questions on school climate, we found the principal's importance mentioned in every category. We wondered what specific behaviors on the part of the school leader are associated with an effective school, and we went back to our original questions to search for possible answers. The questions highlighted three processes of leadership that suggest norms for developing a positive school climate. Specifically, school leaders (1) develop positive models, (2) generate consensus, and (3) use feedback to build a positive school climate. In schools succeeding above expectations, these leadership processes appear to be in place, and they may provide hints about how a school might change if increased student achievement is a valued outcome.

Modeling

We tend to copy the actions, attitudes, and beliefs of people we respect, especially if those people are in positions of authority. Because teachers and administrators hold such positions in a school, their behavior provides important cues to children about what is expected and what is valued there. Let's take a look at how one principal's behavior is perceived by a student hall monitor.

Dr. Black, the principal, is six feet, six inches tall and walks the school's hall with long strides. He makes a definite impression on people, as this passage from a seventh-grader's English composition suggests: "On my way to class, with the halls empty, I was walking behind Dr. Black, who stooped to pick up a piece of paper. He swooped down like an eagle after a field mouse, retrieving the paper without breaking stride. Now, I do the same while thinking of eagles."

Picking up a piece of paper in the hall of a large school is a small gesture, yet it speaks of a person who cares about how the school looks and cares for the people who work and study there. By this one gesture, Dr. Black has modeled a whole constellation of beliefs to the hall monitor. Picking up trash is not seen as a demeaning task but instead is associated in the student's mind with the power of eagles. While most gestures may not be that effective, people in schools do look to respected authority figures for models of appropriate behavior and attitudes. Modeling may be a particularly appropriate way of reinforcing both academic emphasis and an orderly environment.

Let's take a look at the questions that demonstrate the importance of modeling as a leadership process (see Figure 1). We begin by discussing modeling from the perspective of the principal and organize questions to show how modeling can affect a school's climate.

Principals in effective schools model an emphasis on academics by observing classrooms, conferring with teachers about instructional matters, and setting agreed-on goals for the school. "What I do is what I mean," is the way one principal describes his modeling. "If I'm not in those classrooms, then the teachers begin to feel I don't care about the academic program. From observing classrooms, I know the staff's teaching patterns. I know what is being taught. There's less time teaching holiday facts and more time spent on reading and math skills than when I first began in this position. I believe the emphasis of the curriculum changed partly because of our teacher-principal conferences after classroom observations."

Creating and maintaining an orderly environment is enhanced by

Figure 1. Modeling.

The Principal's Role
Modeling for an Academic Emphasis

Does the principal actively set the tone and focus of the school by observing classrooms, enforcing the discipline code in a "fair but firm" manner, and setting goals for the school that are supported by administration, staff, and students?

Does the principal regularly observe classrooms and confer with teachers on instructional matters?

Does the principal emphasize academic standards?

Modeling for an Orderly Environment

Are punishments delivered in a way that indicates firm disapproval of misbehavior while avoiding humiliation and avoiding modeling violence?

Is the building maintained and decorated to provide pleasant working conditions for students?

Is the principal perceived by students and faculty as modeling expectations of fair and equal treatment?

Do high proportions of students hold positions of responsibility?

The Teacher's Role
Modeling for an Academic Emphasis

Do teachers provide rewards for actual achievement?

Do students bring books and pencils to class?

Are staff members willing and available for consultation by children about problems?

Does teacher behavior, such as helping students on the teacher's own time, indicate that the school's children and the profession of teaching are valued?

Modeling for an Orderly Environment

Are positive models of behavior provided by teachers?

Does the faculty express punitive or authoritarian attitudes toward students?

Do teachers start lessons on time and continue without interruption?

Do teachers praise students for work well done?

Do teachers structure the classroom environment to permit students to succeed?

---

the principal's modeling of appropriate behavior for staff and students. This modeling behavior is exemplified in the procedure for determining punishments, the frequency of those punishments, the perceived fairness of the punishments, and the equity with which the punishments are administered to different groups in the school population. Maintaining a well-decorated building where conditions for students are pleasant is another way to demonstrate or model an orderly environment. A clean building suggests order. Modeling by the principal may create an "environmental press" where being orderly is the easiest thing to do.

One way to enhance an orderly environment is to ensure that the school enlists students' participation, not only in the classroom but through having a large proportion of students hold leadership positions in the school. Through participating, the students have a stake in the school.

Teachers—who are, after all, the leaders in the classroom—also model behaviors and attitudes that affect a school's climate. When teachers provide rewards for actual achievement, when students are required to bring books and pencils to class, when teachers are available for consultation outside of the classroom, then teachers are modeling the importance of a school's academic emphasis. A teacher who begins lessons on time is more likely to maintain order in the classroom. Conversely, if students perceive an authoritarian or punitive attitude being modeled by a teacher, they are less likely to internalize the norms of an orderly environment. Teachers also model, by their own behavior, the school's expectations for success. By praising children for work well done, by teaching so that all children experience success, and by spending time on instruction, the teacher communicates these expectations to students.

Of course, modeling can also work in a negative direction. In some low-achieving schools, for example, or in schools with high incidences of violence and vandalism, observers found that teachers did not, as a group, spend the entire class period on academic content. In the same schools, students perceived that a few students could "get away with" inappropriate behavior: "It was only unlucky if you got caught." Such negative models also communicate clearly to school participants.

The models provided by administrators and teachers are one of the keys to leadership in effective schools. The behaviors of teachers and administrators, as authority figures, communicate what is really valued, what is really important in a school.

Consensus Building

Consensus builds as groups of people behave in consistent patterns. At times, these patterns are explicitly agreed on. Schools maintain consistent patterns for beginning and ending the day, for when it is appropriate to talk to the principal, and for when students and teachers eat lunch. Implicit patterns also build, evolving because people begin to behave in a particular way—homework isn't given on weekends, certain groups occupy "their table" in the lunchroom, students don't carry books to classes. Thus, each organization builds consensus patterns, each of which may help or hinder the achievement of the organization's goals. In effective schools, consensus is built around the school climate factors of academic emphasis, orderly environment, and expectations for success. The questions in Figure 2 point to leadership processes that

Figure 2. Consensus Building.

Consensus Building for an Academic Emphasis

Is course planning done by groups of teachers?

Do inexperienced teachers consult with experienced teachers?

Do teachers have extensive contact with a limited number of students in several aspects of their education?

Is there little differentiation among students or in the instructional program provided for them?

Do principals and teachers believe and expect that students can master their academic work?

Consensus Building for an Orderly Environment

Have teachers and administrators come to a working consensus on patterns of acceptable behavior for staff, students, and administration?

Has the principal built shared expectations and strong coordination about school rules?

Do students perceive congruence among the faculty in enforcing school rules and strictly controlling classroom behavior?

Do students perceive that discipline is unfairly administered?

Does there appear to be a working consensus on how school life is organized?

Are there structured opportunities for staff and administration to develop and reinforce consensus?

Consensus Building for Success

Does the social structure of the school teach those who live there that their actions have some effect?

Do students, faculty, administration, and the community feel that their own efforts govern their future?

Do teachers have high expectations for all students, regardless of race or class?

Are there provisions for school outings?

Do a large number of students participate in assemblies?

Do high proportions of students hold positions of responsibility?

Are there out-of-class activities that bring students and teachers together to build toward a common goal?

Does the social structure of the school and classroom provide opportunities for students to practice leadership?

---

may assist in building consensus and developing a positive school climate.

Building consensus for an academic emphasis requires that teachers have time to meet and plan course content together. New teachers need an "old pro" to introduce them to formal and informal school rules and procedures. A consensus emphasizing academics can be destroyed in a few years if new teachers don't understand that students are expected to do their homework in this school and that it's appropriate to require and enforce that students bring books and pencils to class.

The next two questions suggest that a differentiated academic program may have a detrimental effect on creating consensus. In effective schools, there is little differentiation among students' programs. Further, effective schools design schedules that give teachers extensive contact with a limited number of students in several aspects of their education. Ironically, in building an academic emphasis, according to the above criteria, the teacher-student relationship may be more important than a vast smorgasbord of course content. The last question in this area suggests that staff and administration must hold expectations that all students can master the academic content.

In building a consensus for an orderly environment, the idea of a "working consensus" should be emphasized. The staff and administration need to periodically review patterns that promote or disrupt the school's orderly environment. Is a different group of children showing up late for class? Is there a trend in cutting class? Building consensus also means enforcing rules in a consistent manner, so students generally agree that the enforcement is fair and equitable. Arbitrary and inconsistent enforcement of a school's rules leads staff and students to think that luck is a more valued commodity than following the rules.

Students in effective schools feel that their actions have some effect. They believe that if they study, they will get better grades; they know that if they cut school, their parents will be notified. Consensus in this area is likely to bring success in school and a healthy self-concept. School leaders help build this consensus by hundreds of decisions every day.

Consensus can occur only if people interact with one another, however. Thus, success can be fostered by providing for school outings and assemblies and creating opportunities for many students to hold positions of responsibility. Students are likely to be more successful and to have more of an investment in school if they are involved in activities outside the classroom. The idea of student involvement, as described in Chapter 2, takes on additional meaning here. Effective school leadership analyzes patterns of student involvement and opportunities for students to formally exercise responsibility and then seeks improvement in those patterns.

Consensus building is a leadership activity. School leaders in schools with fewer incidents of violence and vandalism than would be expected were able to form a consensus between administration and faculty about both the focus of the instructional program and the disciplinary policies and procedures. It is interesting to note that students were not necessarily involved in developing either consensus. Rather, when students perceived a fair, firm, and consistent consensus on academics and discipline, school outcomes were better than expected. Similarly, Rutter et al. (1979) found a correlation between better student attendance and achievement and teachers who felt their views were considered important by the administration even when they themselves had no actual say in administrative decisions.

Feedback

The school, like all organizations, provides feedback to participants about the acceptability of their behavior. Through feedback, participants learn what is really valued by the organization. For example, most schools have rules about being late for class. Despite such rules, however, in one school almost a third of the students were consistently late for class. Teachers who used to start their classes on time gave up. The students complained when sanctions were imposed and claimed they were imposed inconsistently. After a while, everyone adapted to the situation by starting their classes later. Students understood the feedback the organization provided—it's not important to the school that students get to class on time. The feedback led teachers to understand that students would be late and nothing could be done about it. Another, more subtle, message is that the leadership in this school may not value what happens in the classroom enough to design ways to help get the students to class on time. And the result, of course, was that student involvement, coverage, and success decreased. If eight minutes are lost from each period in an eight-period day, by the end of a 180-day school year, students and teachers will have lost 11,520 minutes or 1,920 hours of time allocated for instruction. No wonder student achievement suffers.

The questions synthesized from the research (see Figure 3) suggest areas where effective school leadership provides feedback that supports a school climate in which academics are emphasized, the environment is orderly, and success is expected.

Both principals and teachers provide feedback that reinforces a school's academic emphasis. Positive feedback to students for a task well done is associated with better student outcomes. It appears obvious that teachers should praise students for work well done, display student work, and regularly give and mark homework. Yet that is not always the case. In many of the ineffective schools covered by case studies, observers found that students were rewarded for incorrect answers or, when they answered correctly, received no reward. Similarly, Rutter et al. (1979) found at least three times as many negative reinforcers as positive ones in the school environment.

Principals provide feedback that supports an academic emphasis by checking to see if teachers give homework, conferring with teachers

Figure 3. Feedback.

Feedback for Academic Emphasis

Do teachers provide rewards for actual achievement?

Do teachers praise students for work well done?

Do teachers praise students' work in class?

Is student work displayed on walls?

Do teachers structure the classroom environment to permit students to succeed?

Do teachers regularly give and mark homework?

Does the principal check to see that teachers give homework?

Does the principal regularly observe classrooms and confer with teachers on instructional matters?

Do teachers and principals support the academic focus of the school by spending most of the school day on instructional activities?

Do teachers feel their views are represented in decision making?

Feedback for an Orderly Environment

Do students perceive congruence among the faculty in enforcing school rules and strictly controlling classroom behavior?

Does the faculty express punitive or authoritarian attitudes toward students?

Do teachers usually handle their infrequent discipline problems themselves?

Are punishments delivered in a way that indicates firm disapproval of misbehavior while avoiding humiliation and avoiding modeling violence?

Is the principal aware of staff punctuality?

Feedback That Builds Expectations for Success

Are rewards earned fairly by a large number of students?

Does the feedback students receive in terms of rewards or praise outnumber punishments?

Do high proportions of students hold positions of responsibility?

Does the social structure of the school and classroom provide opportunities for students to practice leadership?

Is inservice training provided that encourages self-reflection and skill building in areas promoting equal opportunity?

Do students believe that luck is more important than hard work?

Do students believe that they can get ahead without something or someone stopping them?

about instructional matters, and representing teachers' views in the decision-making process.

Students' perceptions of faculty and administration agreement on school rules indicate feedback that reinforces an orderly environment. This feedback avoids humiliation, violence, and authoritarianism, while indicating firm disapproval of misbehavior. Congruence on these matters requires school leaders who are willing to monitor and develop consensus about the way a school operates; when staff punctuality is monitored by administrators, we assume such consensus is developing.

Feedback that builds expectations for success is communicated through rewards and leadership positions for students. When rewards are earned by large numbers of students, when students hold many positions of responsibility, then this feedback supports a climate of success. And when students believe that their actions and decisions can have an impact on their world, success may foster an improved self-concept.

Conclusion

In this chapter we discussed leadership and school climate indicators associated with better school outcomes. The indicators suggest three norms of a positive school climate: an orderly environment, an emphasis on academics, and expectations for success. When grouped another way, the indicators also suggest the three leadership processes of modeling, consensus building, and feedback, which support a positive school climate. Many specific indicators associated with a positive school climate and effective leadership processes are similar to those that lead to student involvement, success, and coverage. Thus, leadership processes and school climate provide one way of understanding what makes a school effective and suggest places where change may significantly affect school outcomes.

6.

Administration and Policy

Perspectives for Effective

Schools

We have reviewed some of the research on characteristics of effective schools and come to the conclusion that effective schools are built on leadership and a positive school climate. Now we would like to illustrate how one principal enhanced the effectiveness of his school by using the ideas of leadership and school climate to focus a school improvement effort. To do this, we first introduce the metaphor of schools as "loosely coupled" systems, hypothesizing that effective schools tend to be more tightly coupled in areas suggested by our model. Next a story is offered to illustrate how Bill's beliefs about leadership and school climate led to changes in student and teacher behaviors that helped improve student achievement. We conclude with a list of implications for superintendents and school boards.

Loose Coupling

During the last 80 years, public schools have mushroomed into ever larger and increasingly more complex institutions. And yet, at the classroom level, the structure of school has hardly changed at all: one teacher meets with 20 to 35 students in a classroom. The difference is that there are more classrooms in schools now.

81

When pieces of an organization, like classrooms, can be added or taken away without substantially affecting the whole, this suggests that the organization is loosely coupled (Weick, 1976; Firestone, 1980). Corbett (1982) defines coupling in this context as "the extent to which action by one person requires or leads to action by another." For example, if there is no relationship between the actions of one classroom and those of another, then a school is considered loosely coupled. If individuals are more interdependent, as in team teaching, the unit is more tightly coupled. A loosely coupled system, in other words, is not like an assembly line where, when one part is lacking, the whole line must shut down.

Schools benefit in many ways from being loosely coupled. Structurally, there needs to be some way to divide children into manageable groups that won't disrupt the school. In no other place in American society are so many people packed into so small an area as children are in schools. For five to six hours a day, 180 days a year, each classroom houses up to 35 students plus a teacher. Small, loosely coupled groups make schools more manageable; if one classroom is chaotic, other classrooms will not be affected.

In a loosely coupled school, one can add or subtract courses in the curriculum and continue school even though teachers, principals, and students change or at times don't perform up to par. Schools can be combined when student enrollment is declining or new ones built when the number of students increases. In a loosely coupled system, internal changes don't have a large impact on the organization as a whole. One Friday afternoon, when the buses were running late, a quarter of the faculty was out on an inservice activity, and the ovens in the cafeteria weren't working, a principal we work with described his school as completely uncoupled. Of course, the fact that all this could happen and school remain in session is one of the positive properties of a loosely coupled system.

In many other ways, however, loose coupling presents problems for a school. Teachers may not know what their colleagues are teaching in the classroom next door. Principals may have difficulty generating consensus on school rules in a large faculty and among a large student body that changes once every three to six years. Given that schools strive toward many different goals, accountability in a loosely coupled school may also be a problem. Coordination may be difficult, as connections between people in the school may rest more on happenstance than on design. As a result, planning in such areas as curriculum may suffer.

Descriptions of effective schools suggest that certain couplings or connections are necessary if schools are to be effective in producing academic achievement. These crucial couplings can help school administrators order their many competing priorities.

The school's schedule of time use is one such area. The time schedule is a plan of how different subunits in a school are coupled or coordinated. Let's use as an example a school where there are four teachers for each grade, 1–4, and two kindergarten teachers. All teachers must have lunch and planning periods during a school day that begins at 8:30 a.m. and ends at 2:45 p.m. Their classes must be scheduled for regular sessions with special teachers in library, art, music, or physical education, who also need lunch and planning time. The six school aides must be equally divided up among the classroom teachers. Provision must be made for serving breakfast to 150 students and supervising the playground and bus loading. And then, the Chapter I teachers need to have access to students who must be pulled out of class for special help—but not during instruction in math and reading. Special education students need to be mainstreamed. There must be special schedules for assemblies and holidays, and a schedule for bathroom breaks and recess.

The image presented here is one of a tightly coupled environment that is constrained by time. The schedule is tight, usually figured to the minute. Such coupling, while necessary, may not be sufficient to produce student achievement above expectations.

Although it is easy to understand why many principals get seduced into spending most of their time managing such a situation (and schools do need full-time management), we suspect that simply managing it is not enough. The school effectiveness research gives us hints about what else is important. Effective schools have time for teachers to plan and meet together, time for systematic supervision of classes, time for students to cover the content that is tested. From case studies of leaders of effective schools, it appears that they are able to structure at least some of their time in these areas.

What we are suggesting is that there are ways to manage efficiently—to run the organization smoothly—while ensuring that a school is also effective; that it produces high student achievement through coupling the "right" areas: student success, involvement, and coverage. The criterion of effective management should not be how well a principal maintains the school's time schedule, although that is important. Rather, the criterion should be promoting student success, involvement, and coverage—the benchmarks of an effective school.

In the following story, the principal's goal is to ensure high engagement and coverage of appropriate academic content. The story describes this principal's attempt to couple his organization around engagement and coverage.

Bill's Story

When I first accepted the position of principal, each wing of the school was running a separate K-4 program, using different texts and different teaching strategies. The three wings were very competitive, each claiming superior results and philosophy. Children were selected for each wing on the basis of a draft. The wings were led by a head teacher in charge of purchasing and staff supervision. The head teachers met with the superintendent as a group; even though I was the principal, I was not involved. It took me almost six months to figure out what exactly was going on in each wing of the school.

One wing had a nongraded philosophy where students progressed through the curriculum at their own pace. Another wing grouped everyone within the grade according to ability and then had all kids change groups about six to eight times a day. Teachers in that wing taught only certain subjects. The third wing had self-contained classrooms for reading and math, but the rest of the subjects were divided among the teachers, each of whom saw all the students. The halls in each wing were always full. I really couldn't tell exactly where kids were if their parents wanted to find them. That's not a happy situation for a principal.

In the beginning, if a parent asked me to describe the school program, I couldn't do it. And when I could, it was complicated and contradictory. At one point, I remember trying to explain why one child, whose mother thought she should be going to middle school, was destined to spend another year at the primary school. It turned out that the girl had repeated second grade, but the system was so unclear that her mother never realized it. The girl herself had no clue either, as the situation was ungraded.

Consensus Building

It seemed to me that the school's professional staff needed to build a consensus around the goals and direction of the school. We formed committees—led by the head teachers and myself and centered around the subject areas of reading, math, social studies, and science—to determine what essentials all children should master. I used the state's minimum competency program as a base, along with four or five of the texts used in the various wings. We also took a look at the standardized test specifications. After a year, we had a list of units with objectives in each subject that almost everyone agreed children should master. By focusing on content areas, the staff became more tightly coordinated.

During the day, the wings had 45 minutes for group planning, led by the wing leaders, while their children went to gym, music, library, or art. After discussion with the wing leaders, we moved to a grade-level plan, where the wing leaders became grade-level leaders. We tried this out initially when the committees met to decide units and objectives for each grade level. During the second year, after discussion with the team leaders, I switched everyone into self-contained classrooms with one* teacher teaching the four major subjects to one group of students. We kept the planning time for the grade-level teams, as we needed to build a new consensus with these groups. The leaders of each wing now shouldered the leadership for grade-level meetings. After a few months they reported that the team meetings concentrated on curriculum, as everyone now had the same curriculum content to teach. The system now focused on teaching agreed-on standard curriculum, and not everyone was pleased with this change. However, I figured that it's easier to coordinate curriculum and instruction within grade levels, rather than having three wings, each with their separate way of doing business. In addition, this system encouraged teachers to take responsibility for a particular group of children and their learning. After a year, not as many students were getting lost between the cracks in the curriculum.

Feedback

Now that the professional staff agreed on the objectives students should master, I asked teachers to schedule when they would cover the objectives. Then I monitored their lesson plans to see that they were keeping up with their schedules, so that all students would have an opportunity to cover the material everyone had decided was important—the material that was on the standardized tests.

This year, I had a way of tracking coverage, as teachers turned in their mastery tests on each objective. Then I compared the dates they completed the units to their schedule of objectives. Most were able to keep up or catch up when they fell behind. I think it had something to do with my knowing where each teacher was and showing I was concerned.

The grade-level leaders and other teachers on the grade-level team provided feedback that reinforced our consensus about what children should master. The grade-level groups discussed instructional strategies and did daily problem solving centered around teaching and individual students. Most groups tend to plan together, and a few teams are now submitting group lesson plans. The group leaders report that they feel more successful because their roles are more closely linked to decisions about curriculum and instruction. This feedback helps to reinforce our school's academic emphasis.

Discipline presented problems when I took over the school, but the problems were reduced when everyone changed to self-contained classrooms. Students were no longer in the halls so much of the time, and individual teachers had responsibility for a limited number of students. But we also developed a consistent set of rules for the school during the second year. We took a day in the summer to list routines kids were expected to follow for such classroom activities as sharpening pencils, going to the bathroom, getting and putting back instructional materials, and changing groups. This was one of the first activities the teachers completed as grade-level teams. The teams developed games to teach children these classroom management skills.

We also reviewed the rules with students through a demonstration. During the first couple of days of school, I stopped by each teacher's classroom to see how the program was being carried out. I believe that providing clear feedback to students on the rules, developing consensus about the rules, and making sure everyone received feedback on their implementation may have contributed to fewer discipline problems.

Modeling

When I took the job as principal, I had an image of the kind of school I wanted—almost a feeling that I carried around inside my head. Of course, the trick is to forge the everyday life of the school so it matches the image. Every month I try to put my excess energies into making reality more like my image.

By being firm and decisive, I try to set a businesslike tone that communicates, "We are here to learn and to teach. We know what it is that students are expected to learn. We know that order is necessary for children to learn. We're proud to be part of an organization that is succeeding and improving." Those four sentences summarize my own image about what a school should be and what I am trying to mold this school toward.

I try to use myself as a model for others. I work longer hours than most, and I build regular classroom visits into my schedule. Once a month I meet with grade-level groups of teachers during planning time to discuss problems and possibilities for the future. At lunch time, I spend a few minutes chatting with staff, while making sure order is maintained in the cafeteria. Faculty meetings center around program improvement and sometimes use the talents of our own staff. Reviewing and commenting on lesson plans and on teachers' and students' success in mastering objectives receive top priority one afternoon a week. While each of these activities overlaps with the next, the redundancy provides me with the knowledge I need to keep tabs on what is happening in the school. I do a lot of listening.

School Climate and My Beliefs

I believe a school should be a safe place where children go about the interesting business of learning in an orderly environment, a school with an academic emphasis and expectations for success. I believe that the leader of a school, usually the principal, creates the school environment. And creating an environment for learning depends on putting your time where your mouth is.

For me, there is a hierarchy of needs to attend to. First, I am concerned about an orderly environment. Is the school safe? Are children physically safe? I keep tabs on the playground, the cafeteria, the classrooms to look for things like spilled food kids could slip on, loose tiles, holes kids could trip in. But my idea of safety goes beyond just the physical. I try to find out whether kids feel safe in the restrooms, on the playing fields, in the locker rooms, in the gym, coming and going from school, and most important, in the classrooms. I keep records of fights and office referrals and sit down once a month to take a look at developing patterns to make sure the kids, their teachers, and, at times, their parents get help from grade-level teams or others in resolving those problems.

Is the school environment orderly? I look for teachers and students being quiet in the halls during classes; between classes a friendly jostle is one thing, but no running or pushing. The teachers know I expect this and do a fine job. In the classrooms, a busy buzz is not uncommon, and I look to see if students are engaged and if the teacher is providing appropriate materials and classroom routines. For beginning teachers and those having difficulty maintaining order, I spend extra time supervising in their classrooms and conferencing with them afterwards. Grade-level leaders and their teams help new teachers understand the school's routines, so most new teachers make a smooth transition. I also check my own management to see what decisions I make that may disrupt school routines, such as use of the intercom, frequent school-wide assemblies, and scheduling such things as special area teachers, substitutes, and physical exams.

Is success expected? All students can succeed if given the time, the appropriate material, and the support and structure they need. I monitor report cards, teachers' unit test results, and standardized tests carefully to determine patterns of success in each class. While in classrooms, I check to see whether teachers are giving all children opportunities to participate, or spending more time with some kids and less with others, or just ignoring some kids. Grade-level leaders share with their teams strategies for increasing student success through increasing teacher interaction with all students. I try to listen carefully when teachers talk about their "problem" students, looking for evidence that the teacher has found ways to use some of each problem student's abilities and attitudes to help ensure that student's success.

I also take a look at how my own behavior supports students' and teachers' success. A supervisory system built on student engagement, content coverage, and success is one way I hope to ensure that the school is effective. Through modeling, feedback, and consensus building, the beliefs I hold about schools are becoming more of a reality. The norms of a safe and orderly environment with an academic emphasis are now widely held; as a school, we all appear to be reading off the same script.

Implications for Superintendents and School Boards

In our review of research on effective classrooms and schools, we found little attention paid to the superintendent, the central office staff, and the school board. Indeed, in some cases, schools were effective because they buffered themselves against "interference" from the district's influence and requirements. This suggests that many school systems may be very loosely coupled, with little coordination between individual schools and their programs. In such systems, effective schools may be created by dynamic principals, but ineffective schools go unchecked. Where that is the case, superintendents and school boards need to create management and policy structures that will couple the school system internally for increased student achievement.

School boards and superintendents set the long-term direction of a school system. They control powerful organizational incentives, such as management structure and objectives, compensation plans, promotion criteria, accountability systems, and planning designs. Unfortunately, however, not all school systems gear these incentives to enhanced student achievement: at times, promotions result from lack of performance on the administrator's part; teacher planning time is reduced in times of austerity; raises are based on longevity rather than merit.

When the board and the superintendent have developed a consensus on the school system's focus, on the other hand, then the organization is more likely to be structured so that student achievement increases. Coupling school systems for increased achievement requires attention to the following policy and management areas:

1. School district philosophy. That musty document needs to be reviewed and perhaps rewritten to show that student achievement is to receive priority in the school district, if this is the consensus of the board and superintendent.

2. Policy analysis. The policy manual should be reviewed to determine which procedures support student success, involvement, and coverage. Research reviewed in previous chapters suggests that the individual school may need more autonomy in hiring staff and expending funds if it is to be effective. Conversely, more accountability of administrators and teachers may need to be built into job descriptions, evaluations, and salary schedules.

3. Goal setting. The school board and superintendent need to reach a consensus not only that student achievement is important, but that it can be improved. Goals for the district should center around that improvement. (See Appendix 2 for an example from Kent, Washington, School District No. 415.)

4. Financial structure. The district's financial structure should be reviewed to determine how its policies and procedures impact on student involvement, coverage, and success. For example, if staff development is a centralized function funded through the central office, then it is not likely that such money will address all schools' individual needs for increasing student involvement, success, and coverage. Instead, the schools may need line items in their budgets for staff development to support changes deemed appropriate at the school level. Acquisition of curriculum material and equipment could be funded in a similar fashion.

5. Accountability. The superintendent should be held accountable to the board, not only for how district funds are spent, but also for student achievement. A quarterly report on student involvement, success, and coverage should be considered as important as a financial statement. The school board should go on record as being accountable to local citizens for improving student achievement. The superintendent should be held accountable by the board for principals' performance.

6. Speed of results. Change happens relatively slowly. The changes we describe would take most school systems a minimum of five years to implement, and longer in larger school systems.

7. Superintendent's contract. The average term of a superintendent's contract is approximately three years. Ironically, substantial changes in schools take much longer. School boards that want consistent leadership should consider longer term contracts with superintendents.

8. Teacher contracts. Contracts between the board and the teachers association should be reviewed to determine which provisions help or hinder student involvement, success, and coverage. The length of the teaching day, planning time, staff development, curriculum development, sick leave, and termination procedures could all impact on student achievement. In some cases, adequate student involvement may hinge on a longer teaching day with provision for teacher planning time.

Summary

How a school system is run gives messages about what is important. A school that is loosely coupled may not engage students successfully enough so that they fulfill the school's expectations. A loosely coupled school may have no organizational press for achievement. On the other hand, effective schools tend to be coupled or coordinated to produce student achievement. In our story, Bill used the three leadership processes of consensus building, feedback, and modeling in building a school that is instructionally coupled. Brief suggestions about the role of superintendents and school boards in helping to develop instructionally coupled schools concluded the chapter. The next chapter focuses on assessing the effectiveness of your own school.

7.

Assessing

School Effectiveness

The indicators of effective schools and classrooms that we have discussed are specific and, in most cases, measurable. For those who want to assess their own schools or school systems, we offer a questionnaire in this chapter that summarizes these indicators of effectiveness. The questions are organized according to the major categories of our model: student behaviors, teacher behaviors, supervision, school climate, leadership, and student achievement.

The questions appear in the first column of the questionnaire. Following each question, in parentheses, is an index to the pages on which more information about the question can be found. The remaining five columns are for respondents to enter comments about the question.

In the second column, each question should be answered by indicating "Y" (yes) or "N" (no). The next column asks for an indication of how certain you are of your response: "0" is completely uncertain and "5" is completely certain. Naturally, not everyone in a school system can be certain about all the questions asked here. Where there appears to be consensus about the certainty or uncertainty of a particular response, these data may give clues about areas where more data are needed. Again, the questionnaire is set up so that you are the judge of the meaning of patterns in the data.

The column headed "What Data Do You Have?" is the most important. Here you are to indicate the kind of data that allowed you to answer the question "yes" or "no." This information may come from your experience as a teacher in a particular classroom or as administrator of a particular school. Or it may come from such sources as lesson plans, logs of classroom interaction, calendars, evaluation reports, hearsay, or rumor. Try to be as specific as possible, for it may be important to know where some people get their data. Principals may get their data from teachers' plans, for example, while school board members may get theirs from parents or students they happen to know. Such sources may point to ways to systematize the school's data-gathering and reporting systems so that consensus is generated by everyone's having similar information.

In the next column, indicate who is responsible for the task or function in question. If you know who is responsible, write in that person's title; if no one is responsible, write in "no one." Finally, in the last column write in the title of the person who checks to make sure the responsible person is carrying out the responsibility. If no one performs such checks, write in "no one." Figure 1 shows how one principal filled out the first question.

Of necessity, the questions are quite general. For example, question 6 asks, "On the average, do students experience high levels of success in their daily work?" A precise answer to this question would require a knowledge of what happens in each classroom and at each grade level in each school. While we aren't suggesting that this information be collected on a systematic basis all the time, it might be interesting to check such data occasionally, especially in light of the great range of success on academic tasks that has been documented in previous studies. For example, the principal might ask for all teachers to report on how the students in their classes did on Friday's spelling test, or how

Figure 1. Sample Response to the Questionnaire.

	Answer Y/N	Certainty 0–5	
Student Behaviors *Involvement:* 1. On the average, is reading/language arts scheduled for at least two hours a day in elementary school? (10-12, 14-15, App. 1)	Y	5	

What Data Do You Have?	Whose Responsibility?	Who Checks?	
School schedule Teachers' lesson plans (except kindergarten)	Principal Teacher	Principal	

many children are failing English year after year, as possible ways to answer that question.

Some people we have shared the questions with were amazed that anyone would even want to question such things: "Most people take these things for granted." Whether most students are involved with academic work for most of the school day, for example, seems like a question it should not be necessary to ask in a school. Unfortunately, such obvious questions do need to be addressed. We believe that most schools will find such an exercise very confirming, however, because most schools are doing well on many of these indicators. The school administrators or supervisors who can answer most of these questions with a high degree of confidence are those who have designed effective management and supervision systems. For them, such questions and their answers will confirm their hard work and may suggest further areas for improvement. The answers may also indicate where the system can be more tightly coupled or coordinated.

Don't think that change strategies will be implemented quickly, however. As our next chapter indicates, it takes time to build an effective school. Organizational change happens over a three- to five-year period, so we suggest that, to start with, a staff should choose only one change area where success appears likely. The more difficult areas can be tackled in later years.

Using the Questionnaire

This questionnaire will work best when it is used by small groups of people who are concerned with student achievement. We suggest that groups interested in using the questionnaire begin with the student behavior questions, as these are most closely linked with student achievement. Three scenarios are suggested:

● **Scenario 1: school level.** At a faculty meeting, the research on student involvement, coverage, and success can be summarized. Then members of the faculty and administration fill out the questionnaire for the first seven questions. Results are tabulated according to grade level, and patterns across grade levels are generated as each grade level reports its findings. After the faculty meeting, grade-level representatives meet with the principal to discuss implications for program modification. When this is completed, another faculty meeting is held to review the research and answer the set of questions on teacher behaviors. Such a scenario may be most effective where schools are not strongly coordinated by a central office and each school has a high degree of autonomy and control over resources.

● **Scenario 2: district level.** For those districts that would like to take a look at how the district management structure influences school effectiveness, we recommend the following scenario. At a meeting of the management team (principals, relevant central office administrators, and the superintendent), participants review research on the particular dimension where change could most easily occur. They then fill out the questionnaire in that area, discern patterns across schools in the district, and generate implications for change.

● **Scenario 3: school board level.** The school board has a vital role in setting the general direction of the district. This questionnaire can be useful to the board in hiring the next superintendent. For example, question 4 on the questionnaire can be turned into an interview question: "How will you be able to assure the school board that students are covering the content and skills measured by our standardized tests?" By using such a question, the board not only gets an indication of the candidate's competence, but also gives the message that student achievement is important. School boards and superintendents can also use the questions to help set priorities for the coming year. Priorities can be set during a planning session at which board members are asked to rank the questions in the order of their importance for improvement during the coming year. The questionnaire then gives the superintendent and other administrators a structured way to look at the school district.

The questionnaire should be used as a process helper, focusing attention on significant questions but leaving it to the participants to decide what areas to collect data on and what the patterns in the data mean. Even the extensive research reported here is not strong enough to provide definitive standards in *all* areas for *all* schools. On the other hand, the areas delineated by the questions *do* have significance for all schools that want to improve their effectiveness.

The data generated by the questionnaire may be threatening to some members of a school's organization. A school board member we met outside a conference session with the title, "Is Your School Effective?" said he was frightened by the question and wasn't sure he really wanted to know the answer. A principal we spoke to responded, "How am I supposed to pay attention to all those questions and still run the school?" Another board member commented, "Now I have something to ask the superintendent next time we decide about his raise." Underlying these responses is a potential for conflict that can surface using this questionnaire. At the center of the conflict is what makes a school effective, and this is an important idea to debate. We would also like to emphasize that there seem to be no universal prescriptions that are appropriate for all classrooms, all schools, or all districts. Rather, research and experience point to a number of areas that should receive focused attention when school or classroom effectiveness is an issue.

Despite any conflicts that might arise, the data generated by the questionnaire should be used to enhance the school's effectiveness. One way to analyze that data is to look for patterns of response. Three such patterns are:

• **Pattern 1.** Everyone answers "yes" to the question, cites similar data sources, names the same people as responsible, and agrees on who does the checking. If the data listed are similar to what is found in the research, then this pattern probably indicates that the school is effective when it comes to that particular question, or that a consensus has developed in this area.

• **Pattern 2.** Answers in the "yes/no" column are inconsistent. People cite different data sources and are unclear about who is responsible and who should check. This pattern may indicate that the formal organization pays little attention to this particular area. Or, it may indicate that different people perceive the answers in different ways, which suggests the need for further discussion, building toward consensus.

• **Pattern 3.** Everyone answers "no" and leaves blanks in many other columns. A consensus of "no" answers may indicate that the school or district is ignoring one of the factors that may lead to a more effective school.

After the data are collected and analyzed, priorities for change should be focused on those areas most likely to influence student achievement. In our model, those areas are student and teacher behaviors. Of course, management systems need to be in place to ensure the efficiency of any change. And the school board needs to understand and support the process if long-term improvement is sought. Such change is the central theme of the following chapter.

Questionnaire for Assessing School and Classroom Effectiveness.

	Answer Y/N	Certainty 0–5	What Data Do You Have?	Whose Responsibility?	Who Checks?
Student Behaviors *Involvement:*					
1. On the average, is reading/language arts scheduled for at least two hours a day in elementary school? (10-12, 14-15, App. 1)					
2. On the average, is math scheduled for 50 minutes a day in elementary school? (10-12, 14-15, App. 1)					
3. Are most students involved most of the time? (3-4, 10-11, 14-15, 22-23, 54, 57-58, 64-65, 67, 69-70, App. 1)					
Coverage:					
4. Are students covering the content and skills measured by the outcome measure? (3-4, 11-15, 22-23, App. 1)					
5. Have students mastered the prerequisites before working on new skills? (11-13, 15-16)					
Success:					
6. On the average, do students experience high levels of success in their daily work? (3-4, 13-15, 21-23, 60, App. 1)					
7. On the average, do students master most of the content covered in reading/language arts and math? (13-16, 66-67)					

Teacher Behaviors

Planning:

8. Do teachers, early in the year, plan for the content to be covered during the year? (5, 16-17)

9. Do teachers plan, in advance, so that materials and activities are closely linked to the objectives and goals by which the program is evaluated? (16-17, 57-59, 64, 67)

10. Do teachers have and use data on prior achievement of their students? (3, 16-17)

11. Have teachers prepared plans for developing classroom management before the first day of school that include:
   —analyzing classroom tasks
   —identifying expected behaviors
   —developing ways to teach rules and procedures? (5, 17-19)

12. Do teachers plan for and expect students to succeed? (5, 49, 52, 54, 57-59, 61, 63, 71, 74)

13. Are classroom disruptions infrequent? (57-59, 69-70)

Classroom Management:

14. Does the teacher ensure that transition from one activity to another is done with a minimum loss of instructional time? (18, 57-59)

15. Are all students provided approximately equal opportunity to respond and become involved in instruction? (52, 57-58, 62)

	Answer Y/N	Certainty 0–5	What Data Do You Have?	Whose Responsi-bility?	Who Checks?
16. Does the teacher consistently enforce the classroom rules and procedures so discipline problems are infrequent? (18-19, 51, 57-58, 60-64, 69-70, 74, 75, 79)					
17. Does the teacher start lessons on time and continue without interruption? (57-59, 67)					
Instruction: 18. Do teachers spend sufficient time presenting, demonstrating, and/or explaining new content and skills to the whole group of students in the classroom? (5, 19-21, 23, 57-59, 62, 64, 67)					
19. Are the teacher's explanations and directions clear and understandable? (19-20, 64)					
20. Do teachers provide adequate opportunity for students to practice and reinforce newly acquired skills and content where help is available? (19-20, 57-58, 60)					
21. Do teachers monitor students' performances and provide constructive feedback, as needed? (18, 20, 54)					
22. Do teachers assign independent practice activities such as seatwork and homework only after students have demonstrated understanding of a skill or concept? (20, 57-59, 79)					

23. Do teachers use a system for monitoring and recording achievement of instructional objectives? (20-21, 59)

Supervision
24. Does the principal regularly observe classroom instruction? (54-55, 63-64)

25. Does the principal meet regularly with teachers to discuss classroom practices? (54-55)

26. Has the school, as an organization, specified procedures and criteria for evaluating instructional personnel that focus on student management, success, and coverage? (25-28, 60-61, 74)

27. Have principal and staff received training in procedures of evaluating and supervising so that principal and staff know about the rules under which supervision and evaluation are conducted? (28-30, 63-64)

28. Do conflicts inherent in the supervising and evaluating process surface from the viewpoint of the principal and teachers? (30-44)

29. Are the data patterns recorded during supervision and evaluation related to valued outcomes such as student engagement, success, and coverage? (5-6, 26-27, 54-55)

School Climate
Academic Emphasis:
30. Do students expect to and actually master the academic work? (19, 49, 52, 54, 57-58, 61-62, 71)

	Answer Y/N	Certainty 0-5	What Data Do You Have?	Whose Responsibility?	Who Checks?
31. Do teachers and principal support the academic focus of the school by spending most of the day on instructional activities? (5-6, 23, 54-55, 57-58, 66-67, 78-79)					
32. Do teachers give and mark homework? (5-6, 57-60, 79)					
33. Do teachers reward and reinforce actual achievement? (52, 54, 74, 78-79)					
34. Is academic learning the primary focus of the school? (63-65, 79)					
Orderly Environment: 35. Do students perceive congruence among the faculty in enforcing school rules and strictly controlling classroom behavior? (6, 51, 57-58, 61-67, 69-71, 74, 76-77, 79-80)					
36. Do a large majority of students hold positions of responsibility, participate in schoolwide activities, use the library, and care for school resources? (52, 57-59, 61-62, 66-67, 69, 77-79)					
37. Are punishments delivered in a way that indicates firm disapproval of misbehaviors while avoiding humiliation and avoiding modeling violence? (51, 59-60, 74, 76, 79)					
38. Are teachers available to consult with students about problems? (57-61)					

Expectations for Success:

39. Do students feel the school helps them to master the academic work? (49, 52, 54, 57-58, 61, 63-64, 77, 79, 87-88)

40. Do principal and teachers believe and expect all students, regardless of race or class, to master the academic work? (6, 54, 61, 63-64, 70-71, 76)

41. Do students believe that work is more important than luck in order to succeed? (49, 52, 54, 57-58)

Modeling:

42. Are positive models of behavior provided by teachers and administrators? (6, 59, 63-64, 73-76)

43. Do teachers praise students for work well done? (18, 52, 54, 57-58, 60, 67-68)

44. Is the principal perceived by staff and students as modeling the expectation of fair and equal treatment? (63-65, 73-74)

Consensus Building:

45. Is course planning done by a group of teachers? (57-58, 60-61, 68, 76-77)

46. Do high proportions of students hold positions of responsibility? (52, 57-59, 62, 69)

47. Do teachers have extensive contact with a limited number of students in several aspects of their education? (19, 50, 54)

	Answer Y/N	Certainty 0–5	What Data Do You Have?	Whose Responsibility?	Who Checks?
48. Have teachers and administrators come to a working consensus on patterns of acceptable behavior for staff, students, and administrators? (6-7, 50-52, 54-55, 57-58, 61, 65, 68, 75-77, 84-85)					
49. Does the school teach those who work and learn there that they can get ahead without something or someone stopping them? (49, 52, 54, 57-59, 64, 68, 71, 87-88)					
Feedback:					
50. Do teachers provide rewards for actual achievement and praise students for work well done? (18, 51, 54, 57-59, 67)					
51. Does the principal regularly observe classrooms and confer with teachers on instructional matters? (54-55, 63-64)					
52. Do teachers feel their views are represented in decision making? (61, 64, 68, 78)					
53. Does the feedback students receive in terms of rewards and praise outnumber punishments? (51, 57-58, 60)					
54. Does the principal provide a reliable system of support, appropriate inservice training for staff, and opportunities for staff to coordinate their actions in the areas of instruction and discipline? (6, 51-52, 54-55, 57-58, 63-64, 78-80, 85-86)					

Student Achievement

55. Are achievement tests used to evaluate attainment of basic skills? (3, 7-8, 16-17)

56. Do students from poorer families achieve as well as students from middle-class families? (3, 48-49, 52-54, 63)

57. Are standardized achievement test results reported in usable form to:
    —students
    —teachers
    —administrators
    —school board members
    —community? (16, 88-90)

58. Has the school board set student achievement as a major goal for the school system? (88-90, App. 2)

59. Do management and instructional systems exist that support student achievement? (54-55, 57-58, 63-64, 78-80)

60. Are the results of achievement tests used to modify the curriculum or instructional programs? (3, 7-8, 16-17)

8.

Principles of the

Improvement Process

In previous chapters we reviewed research relating to effective classrooms and schools and identified a relatively few essential characteristics that differentiate more and less effective schools. We also suggested how principals, superintendents, and school boards can use this information to improve schools under their control.

The purpose of this chapter is to offer a few guidelines for school improvement efforts taken from research and from our experience. These guidelines are not intended as an in-depth review or synthesis, and readers are referred to Emrick and Peterson (1978), Lehming and Kane (1981), Pincus and Williams (1979), and Zaltman, Florio, and Sikorski (1977) for more complete reviews.

Berman (1981) has identified three stages of the improvement process: mobilization, implementation, and institutionalization. The problems faced in each of these three stages are different, as are the expected outcomes. Therefore, our suggestions are grouped under these three rubrics.

Mobilization

Mobilization, or getting started, includes such activities as planning, assessing needs, setting an agenda, determining resources, and creating awareness. Of course, one of the most important activities is the decision to actually adopt an innovation or begin a change effort. Three guidelines should be kept in mind regarding the mobilization process: (1) the innovation should be a long-range, focused effort; (2) an

104

appropriate entry point must be selected; and (3) the central role of the principal must be considered.

Plan a Long-Range, Focused Effort

Too often, we want a quick fix. We believe a three-hour inservice session (or better yet, a one-hour session) will solve our problems. Solutions should be easy, painless, and cheap, we think. But guess what? That's not the way it is. School improvement takes time and hard work. It may even cost money.

Our experience suggests that anyone attempting to make more than a minor change should plan on three to five years for implementation. We don't know why that idea is foreign to so many superintendents. Most districts have five-year plans for equipment replacement—why not for instruction? Note that in the vignette in Chapter 1 the principal is reflecting on three years of effort. Imagine if the changes he made had all been attempted in one year.

To fully implement activities that will create the characteristics we described earlier (if most of them are not already present) requires a long-range, sustained effort. Changing behavior and changing norms takes time. One change project found that just trying to improve communication skills in a faculty is counterproductive unless more than twenty-four hours of training is provided (Runkel and Schmuck, 1974).

In addition to having a long-range perspective, the improvement process should also be focused. Fullan and Pomfret (1977) found that innovations are more likely to be successful if the goals are discrete and moderately complex. Under the model presented in this monograph, the ultimate goal is the improvement of student achievement; short-range goals would be changes in the dimensions affecting student achievement (that is, student behavior, teacher behavior, supervision, school norms and values, and school leadership).

Change in any one of these dimensions might be considered a major innovation in and of itself. Therefore, it is probably unwise to focus on all of the dimensions in one year. Rather, the entire model might be presented and one or two dimensions targeted as the focus for getting started. Then, as the staff becomes proficient in one skill, a new dimension can be targeted.

In fact, our experience shows that each of the student behaviors might best be treated as a separate change area. We have found that teachers can be enthusiastic about learning the skills involved in observing and improving student involvement. But when the schedule requires training on coverage before teachers feel comfortable and proficient in the first area, they become frustrated.

The importance of having a clear and shared focus for the whole effort—somewhat akin to the "image" mentioned in an earlier chapter (Reinhard et al., 1980)—cannot be overemphasized. All the staff should be able to see a picture of what their school will be when the effort has borne fruit. As we said earlier, the model combining classroom and school factors provides an organizing framework to tie together various improvement activities. Moreover, staff must understand how these various activities contribute to reaching that goal. They must see how both increasing time-on-task and analyzing test content can lead to improved student achievement. This will help avoid the all-too-prevalent feeling that change is being made for the sake of change or that the staff must put up with a new fad each year. We have heard many teachers say, "There's no need to take this seriously. Next year they'll want us to try something else." If the staff understands the goal, they are more likely to accept and support the work involved.

Select an Appropriate Entry Point

Given that the improvement process will take more than one year and that everything can't be started at once, it is important to select an appropriate entry point. One crucial consideration is whether the staff perceives an important problem or an "opportunity for improvement" (Havelock, 1970). That is, there may be problems that are not perceived or acknowledged by the staff, but in order to attack those problems you may need to begin with the staff's list. If they see you are willing to help with what *they* believe to be problems, then they are more likely to cooperate in efforts focusing on the problems *you* perceive.

Since the student, teacher, and school-level factors are interdependent, you will often find that a single activity may lead to improvement in more than one area. For example, the process of learning to improve student engaged time usually involves the principal and teachers in communicating about academic goals and learning a common vocabulary to describe a classroom. This often results in the teachers seeing the principal as more concerned about academics and the staff having greater consensus on expectations for teaching. The communication in the training session can also help build more appropriate norms for teacher behavior.

Another consideration is that it may be best not to start with the most severe problem, since solving it may require the most time, work, and skill. Rather, begin on a problem on which there can be some progress rather soon (Havelock, 1970). This success will reinforce the staff for their efforts.

Consider the Role of the Principal

A strong principal is one of the hallmarks of an effective school, and any attempt to make a substantial, lasting impact on a school must involve its principal. This has been shown in repeated studies of school change (Wellisch et al., 1978; Berman and McLaughlin, 1975; Sikorski et al., 1976; Lipham, 1977; Little, 1981). In a recent study of school-based organizational development efforts, Stout and Rowe (1981) found that the single best predictor of success was the principal's estimation, before the project was implemented, of how successful it was likely to be in his or her school. Those principals who predicted failure were not likely to support the innovation. Similarly, in a review of the results of a major study of change conducted by the Rand Corporation, McLaughlin and Marsh (1978) noted that the principal's attitude was critical to the long-term results of change projects. They found that very few of the projects toward which the principal displayed unfavorable attitudes were able to be successfully implemented.

What is it that principals do that makes them so crucial to change efforts? A study by Reinhard (1980) suggests several behaviors by which principals can make an impact. First, they show commitment to the concept and vision of the project at the outset. Second, principals work to achieve role clarity for all the participants. Next, they buffer the staff by negotiating with competing environmental pressures. Then they secure and provide the necessary resources. Finally, they provide social support as well as actively participating themselves. Such behavior seems to endow the concept of leadership with explicit meaning.

But crucial as they are to the change effort, not all principals support innovations. In one district, for example, orientations were scheduled at two schools. At one school, the principal notified teachers well in advance of the after-school meeting and its purpose, had the room and equipment ready, and was on hand to learn and help. At the other, teachers were told only at the last minute to report to the meeting. The room was not arranged adequately, and the principal showed no signs of support. Little wonder that many more teachers in the first school than in the second volunteered to participate.

Implementation

Implementation is the process of actually following through with an innovation. It includes all of the activities necessary to carry out the innovation at a specific site. Two activities that are especially important are adapting the innovation to local circumstances and clarifying the innovation continually as it is being used. Two guidelines seem to be particularly relevant: continually monitor and evaluate the implementation, and complete what you start.

Monitor and Evaluate

Monitoring whether your activities are being carried out as planned and evaluating whether the activities are having the intended effect is essential (Pincus and Williams, 1979; Wellisch et al., 1978). First, if what you planned did not occur, there is no sense in trying to see if it worked. Second, if what was planned was implemented, you need to know if it worked or whether you should try something else. The data-gathering suggestions in Chapters 2 and 4 and in Appendix 1 can provide information for monitoring and evaluation.

Beyond the value of monitoring and evaluation for decision making is their symbolic importance. Conducting these functions honestly sends a clear signal that plans are to be carried out and results are expected.

Finally, evaluation permits public acknowledgment of accomplishments made, thereby reinforcing the effort.

Complete What You Start

Be sure to carry through what you set out to do. If you allow efforts to die or to be continually postponed, you may kill any chance of getting the staff to be serious about future improvement efforts. In one project, for example, each training session that was scheduled was cancelled at the last minute by the principal. Teachers became increasingly frustrated and less willing to continue with follow-up activities between sessions. While reasons for cancelling an activity are often legitimate, the principal should realize the consequences and weigh the alternatives.

Not only must you identify what you are willing to finish, but you must also identify what you have the resources to complete. If a particular activity specifies that 15 hours of inservice training are needed but only 6 hours are left in the school year, it is unrealistic to expect that activity to be completed that year. It may be acceptable to complete only 6 of the 15 hours, but make it clear that this is only one phase and more will follow the next year.

Institutionalization

Institutionalization is the process of stabilizing or establishing new routines as part of the ongoing operation of the system. We offer one guideline relating to the institutionalization stage: move from "project" status to "standard operating procedure" as quickly as possible. As long as a school improvement effort is seen as a project, it is quite vulnerable (Corbett, 1983). The quicker it becomes part of the ongoing operation of the school or district, the more likely it is to endure.

Certainly many of the activities required to implement the improvement effort do not need to be continued. But the critical features of the project must become institutionalized or made a part of the school norms and work behavior. For example, a principal can regularly observe engaged time as part of the routine, ongoing operation of the school. A principal in Delaware does just this (Bailey and Morrill, 1980). She observes each teacher several times a year and includes engagement rate as a regular part of that observation. In the same way, compiling a school year planning guide for academic content can be as routine as compiling absentee lists. In short, these critical activities need to be seen as normal.

Conclusion

The research findings from the previous chapters can serve as the target of school improvement efforts. In other chapters, we have offered suggestions for assessing these critical areas and monitoring any change. We hope that this chapter has offered a few principles of how to put together a general strategy for improvement. It will not be easy or quick, but it can be done.

9.

Summary

Schools can be effective in producing high student achievement, a safe environment, low delinquency, good student behavior, and high attendance regardless of students' socioeconomic status. In effective classrooms, achievement on standardized tests is linked to the amount of time a student actively works on academic content, the amount of content the student covers that is on the standardized test, and the student's success on daily assignments and unit tests.

Student involvement, coverage, and success can be enhanced by teachers' actions in the classroom, by supervisors' and principals' work with teachers, and by school leadership that structures the organization to create a positive school climate. For example, teachers, through planning, classroom management, and instructional procedures, and principals, through their supervision, influence the degree to which students are involved, cover the appropriate content, and succeed in daily assignments and unit tests. These indicators of effective classrooms are also found in the research on effective schools. For example, school leaders can enhance a school's effectiveness by emphasizing academics, promoting an orderly environment, and reinforcing expectations of success. Principals and teachers can create such a positive school climate by modeling appropriate behavior, providing feedback on academics and discipline, and building a consensus about school goals related to achievement and discipline.

While schools can be focused on student involvement, success, and coverage, it is not a simple job. If adequate time is to be spent on basic skills instruction in reading and math, then such instruction will "use up" significant portions of the school day. Teachers and principals face difficult choices in deciding how to allocate time. Schools are experiencing increasing demands for education in a wide variety of subjects, such as family living, vocations, computers, environmental education, and nutrition education, along with subjects already in most school curricula—art, music, shop, physical education, and health. Time, probably more than money, dictates school priorities. Decisions about time allocation aren't new, of course, but more is now known about the relationship of time to student achievement. Curricular decisions can now be more precise, albeit more complicated, because of our knowledge about the impact of student involvement on student achievement.

Similar dilemmas exist for coverage—particularly if one basis for determining adequate coverage is standardized tests. Standardized tests in any subject area do not cover all the essential skills and knowledge in that area. In communications skills, for example, standardized tests cover such skills as reading comprehension of short passages, phonetic analysis, and usage, but often ignore writing, oral language, and an analysis of other media. Using knowledge about the relationship of coverage to student achievement, school leaders can weigh what is important to cover in any curriculum. We have some tools, such as objectives and curriculum alignment procedures, for keeping track of the contents of the school's curriculum. Progress is even being made in mapping the "hidden curriculum" of schools (Bussis, Chittendon, and Amarel, 1976). These tools can assist school districts in focusing their instructional programs. The anecdotes and research summaries from this book contain other suggestions.

If success fosters success, as the research on effective schools and classrooms indicates, then school leaders may want to examine how schools as organizations encourage students' success. Indeed, a number of our nation's schools are organized to screen students so that only the "better" ones remain for further education. The United States has been remarkably successful in educating large numbers of students for a greater number of years than any other country. Nevertheless, the tension continues between sorting students and ensuring that all students master the curriculum. The research cited here suggests that all students *can* master the content and concepts of a school's curriculum.

The research on effective schools points to a school's organization and leadership as major contributors to positive school outcomes. For example, Rutter (1979) found that students who attended effective high schools in inner-city London were less likely to have their names recorded in police records. The schools with lower delinquency rates also had higher attendance, higher achievement, and lower rates of violence and vandalism within the schools. Such evidence leads to the conclusion that schools, as organizations, have a significant effect on students' academic and social lives.

Other studies suggest that the leadership of the school, particularly the principal, plays a critical role in positive school outcomes. Such leaders organize the school so that teachers maximize student involvement and success. Effective schools have leaders who reinforce an academic emphasis, an orderly environment, and expectations for success from students and staff. Leaders reinforce these norms by modeling desired behaviors, providing appropriate feedback, and generating a consensus about the purpose of the school. The questions in Chapter 7 suggest areas that leaders of effective schools have in common.

The research on effective school leadership is strong enough that we can begin using it in planning and performance appraisals of schools and their leaders. Again, this is much more easily said than done. The design of plans and appraisals begs a discussion about what is important for children to learn, for schools to teach, and for a school's leadership to nurture and direct. The successful judgments made in the past can now be bolstered by findings that correlate with school outcomes.

In summary:

1. Research points to questions that can be asked to determine the effectiveness of schools.

2. Measurement of school and classroom effectiveness is possible in terms of both outcomes—such as achievement, attendance, safety, and student behavior—and processes—such as students', teachers', and principals' behaviors of modeling, feedback, and consensus building.

3. Areas that contribute to school effectiveness are under the control of those who structure, direct, and govern the schools.

Findings from the research on effective schools and classrooms are not meant to be used as hammers; they should not be held as ultimate and fixed standards for all schools. On the other hand, they shouldn't be ignored, particularly by schools in which student achievement could improve. These findings provide one way to test individual practices and assumptions about the complex realities of schools against findings that may be more reliable and valid and involve a greater number of schools. This review frames questions for those interested in providing quality education for all children. With these questions, they can test their own circumstances, assumptions, and behaviors while confirming the best of their educational practices.

Appendix 1.

Monitoring Student

Behaviors

In this appendix, we would like to briefly discuss instruments and procedures that can be used to monitor the critical student behaviors of involvement, coverage, and success. These instruments and procedures are adapted from training manuals developed at Research for Better Schools, Inc. (Huitt, Caldwell, Traver, and Graeber, 1981; Segars, Caldwell, Graeber, and Huitt, 1981; see also American Association of School Administrators, *Time on Task: Using Instructional Time More Effectively*).

Involvement

Student involvement is monitored by looking at three factors: allocated time, engagement rate, and student engaged time. We will discuss each one in turn.

Allocated Time

Data on allocated time can be collected by teachers, who simply note the actual (rather than scheduled) beginning and ending time of their lessons and record it on a log such as that shown in Figure A-1.

In this example, Ms. Jones first listed the reading/language arts and mathematics activities she had scheduled for October 2. Then as each activity began and ended, she simply noted the time on the log. At the end of the day, she calculated the time for each activity and then the total allocated time for reading/language arts and math.

Figure A-1. Allocated Time Log.

Allocated Time Log

Teacher   *Ms. Jones*   Date   *10/2*

Reading/Language Arts

Activity	Begin	End	Time
Whole-class instruction	9:01	9:30	29
Seatwork	9:35	9:44	14
Group	10:45	11:45	60
Spelling	1:30	1:41	11
SSR	2:00	2:15	15
			129

Math

Activity	Begin	End	Time
Drill	8:45	8:57	12
Whole-class instruction	9:53	10:10	17
Seatwork	10:10	10:25	15
Groups	1:05	1:27	22
			66

Engagement Rate

Engagement rate data is best collected by an observer other than the classroom teacher (for example, peer teachers or supervisors). One example of how this might be done is included in the chapter on positive supervision (Chapter 3).

Several important points should be considered. First, the observer should talk to the teacher before observing the class to learn what the teacher expects will take place. Next, observer and teacher need to agree on a set of definitions of on-task and off-task behaviors. A number of research studies have generated such definitions. In general, "engaged" simply means being involved in or attending to instruction in the assigned academic content. For example, engaged students may be reading, writing, answering the teacher's questions, watching another student answer a question on the board—or doing anything else that indicates they are involved in the task at hand.

Unengaged students, on the other hand, are not involved in learning academic content. Figure A-2 presents a set of definitions adapted from the Follow Through Evaluation Study (Stallings and Kaskowitz, 1974), which lists five categories of unengaged behavior. The acronym "Ms. Duo" (for Management/transition, Socializing, Discipline, Unoccupied/observing, and Out of the room) has been suggested as an aid in remembering the categories.

Finally, the observer needs to collect data in such a way that the engagement rate can be computed. A simple formula is:

$$\text{Engagement rate} = \frac{\text{Total students engaged}}{\text{Total students observed}}$$

A form that can be used to collect engagement rate data is shown in Figure A-3. In this example, the observer went into the class in the

Figure A-2. Definitions of Unengaged Student Behaviors.

Management/ Transition:	getting ready for instruction, waiting, listening to nonacademic directions, or changing activities
Socializing:	interacting socially or watching others socialize
Discipline:	being reprimanded by an adult, being punished, or watching other students being scolded
Unoccupied/ Observing:	wandering about with no evident purpose or goal, watching other people or unassigned activities, or playing with materials
Out of the Room:	going out of the room temporarily

Figure A-3. Completed Engagement Rate Form.

Engagement Rate Form

State ____ State # ____ School # ____ Subject MATH
District ____ District # ____ Teacher # ____ Part of Class Observed
School ____ Jones Date 10/2 Beg. ✓
Teacher Brown Coder # ____ Mid.
Coder ____ End
Date 10/2 Grade ____ # Students Present

	1	2	3	4	5	6	7	8	9
Time	10:00	10:01	10:02	10:03	10:04	10:05	10:06	10:07	10:08
Assigned	20	20	20	20	20	20	20	20	20
Management/Transition					II	I		I	卌 III
Socializing				II	II				
Discipline									
Unoccupied/Observing	I	II		II	III	II		I	III
Out of Room									
Total Unengaged	1	2	0	4	8	3	0	2	12
Engaged	19	18	20	16	12	17	20	18	8

Time	10 10:09	11 10:10	12 10:11	13 10:12	14 10:13	15 10:14	Total	Engagement Rate $\frac{\text{Engaged}}{\text{Assigned}}$
Assigned	20	20	20	20	20	20	300	
Management/ Transition	卌 卌 卌	卌 | 卌	卌	||	|	|||	49	
Socializing					|||		8	
Discipline	=		卌			卌 |||	13	
Unoccupied/ Observing		卌	|		卌	|	30	
Out of Room								
Total Unengaged	17	16	11	2	10	12	100	
Engaged	3	4	9	18	10	8	200	$\frac{200}{300} = 67\%$

middle of a math lesson and made 15 separate observations at one-minute intervals. On each observation, the observer noted the number of students who were unengaged and made tally marks in the appropriate unengaged categories. At the end of each observation, the observer totaled the unengaged students and calculated the number of engaged students by subtracting the number who were unengaged from the number who were assigned to the task. At the end of the 15 observations, the observer calculated the total number of students who were observed during all the observations and the total number of students who were engaged. Since all students were assigned to math activities during the period of observation, the total observed would be 20 students, multiplied by 15 observations, or 300 student observations. The total number of students engaged would be calculated by simply summing the number of engaged students for all 15 observations, or 200 students.

The engagement rate is then calculated by dividing the total number of students engaged (200) by the total number of students observed (300). In this case, the engagement rate is 67 percent.

Student Engaged Time

The third measure of involvement, student engaged time, is the product of allocated time and engagement rate.

One way for teachers to monitor student involvement is to keep a record of all information collected throughout the year. The summary sheet shown in Figure A-4 is an example of how this might be done.

In this example, Ms. Jones' math class has been observed previously on September 30, and that data has already been entered on the summary sheet. For the October 2 observation, the allocated time of 66 minutes was obtained from the allocated time log shown in Figure A-1. The engagement rate of 67 percent was obtained from the engagement rate form shown in Figure A-3. The student engaged time of 44 minutes, obtained during the October 2 observation, is averaged with the previous data for an average student engaged time of 38 minutes.

Changes in the use of classroom time can be monitored easily by plotting the collected data on a graph. Figure A-5 shows an observation record for student engagement time in third-grade math that has been developed using this data. The vertical axis shows the expected level of achievement based on the reanalysis shown in Figure 2, Chapter 2. The horizontal axis shows the months of the school year. The shaded portion of the graph indicates "at expected level of achievement." In this example, the student engaged time data on the summary sheet shown in Figure A-4, plus data from the rest of the year, have been plotted. It is readily apparent that student engaged time for the first two observation

Figure A-4. Completed Summary Sheet.

State _____   **SUMMARY SHEET**
District _____
School _____   State # _____   School # _____   Subject _MATH_
Teacher _JONES_   District _____   Teacher _____   Year __1981__

Date	Coder #	Part of Period	Engage-ment Rate	Allocated Time	Student Engaged Time	Average Student Engaged Time
9/30	×127	BEG	55%	60 min	33 min	X
10/2	12	MID	67%	66 min	44 min	38 min

days falls in the "below expected" zone. Based on the Stallings and Kaskowitz data, unless things change we would expect this class to perform less well on the upcoming achievement test than might be expected given the students' previous performance.

A major benefit of monitoring the status of student involvement throughout the school year is that corrective action can be taken early if necessary. For example, the engagement rate for students in Ms. Jones' room was about 60 percent for the two days, which is about average when data is collected using the procedures described. It is not unreasonable that the engagement rate could be improved to 80 percent, which would mean that students would spend about twelve minutes more per day than they do now actually involved in mathematics.[1]

Coverage

By coverage we mean that the content students cover during the course

---

[1]80 percent (new average engagement rate) × 63 minutes (average allocated time) = 50 minutes student engaged time; present average student engaged time = 38 minutes.

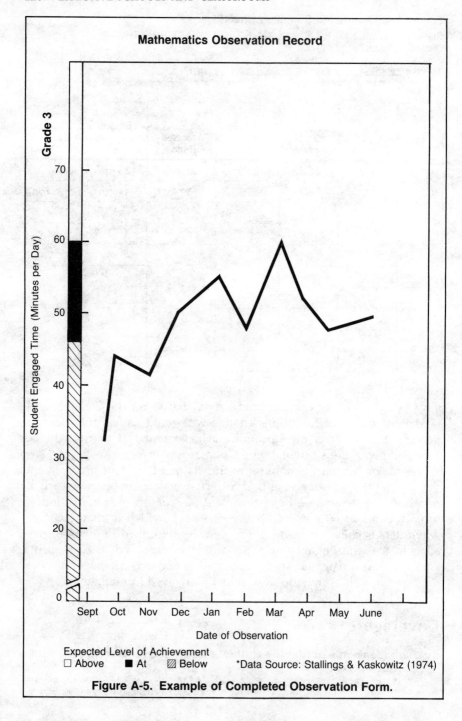

Figure A-5. Example of Completed Observation Form.

of the school year should be appropriate, both in terms of the students' prior learning of the prerequisites and in terms of the content that is to be tested on the standardized achievement test at the end of the year.

Monitoring whether the content covered is appropriate for the students' prior learning is probably best done by looking at the two other student behaviors: engagement rate and success. Students are not likely to work actively on an assignment that is either too easy or too difficult; nor are they likely to be successful on a task for which they don't have the necessary prerequisite skills.

Procedures for monitoring content coverage will vary depending on whether teachers and supervisors follow the procedures suggested in Chapter 2 for aligning curriculum and test content. If a curriculum guide is available that represents an optimal overlap of test topics and local curriculum topics, then teachers and supervisors need only monitor progress through the curriculum guide. A form such as that shown in Figure A-6 can be used by teachers to list the topics and the dates they are covered.

This example shows part of the typical math content for a fourth grade class in the column labeled "Curriculum." The curriculum listed in this guide has been placed according to topics; an alternative arrangement may be to sequence the curriculum in approximately the way it might be taught. In the column labeled "Materials," the district has entered the particular textbook pages that deal with that topic. Where the textbook does not match well with the curriculum, the district has developed a supplementary workbook. In the column labeled "Topics on Current Test," the district has indicated whether that particular content is on the test and what format is used. The district has also provided a guide to the average number of days needed to teach that content. The total number of days needed for this content is thought to be about 150 days, leaving room for the teacher to add additional topics as desired. The teacher has listed the relative strengths and weaknesses of his or her students in the column labeled "Prior Learning." This information might be obtained from the previous year's achievement test results (if testing was done in the spring) or through diagnostic testing at the beginning of the school year. In the column labeled "Date/Success," the teacher has listed the date on which instruction and testing on that topic were completed for the majority of students and the number of students who were successful on that date.

Supervisors can review these forms periodically (perhaps every nine weeks) to determine if the rate of coverage is adequate. They should not try to impose a lockstep curriculum that requires every teacher to be on the same page at the same time, however. Flexibility is needed, but the goal of teaching students what they need to know must

Figure A-6. Sample Page from School Year Planning Guide.

School Year Planning Guide
Mathematics—Grade 4

Whole Numbers	Curriculum	Materials	Topics on Current Test	Prior Learning	Days Needed	Date	Success
	Numeration/Place Value Place value to million	Houghton Mifflin pp. 22–29	Place value to ten thousands Renaming numbers		3	9-21	10 of 25
	Roman numerals to 100	Houghton Mifflin p. 44 Supplementary workbook pp. 4–5			2	9-21	12 of 25
	Addition & Subtraction Facts	Houghton Mifflin pp. 2–16		Strength-Addition	4	9-21	24 of 25
	Regrouping up to ten thousands place	Houghton Mifflin pp. 47–69 Supplementary workbook pp. 15–18	Up to 5 digits, vertical and horizontal formats	Weakness	4	10-9	15 of 25

Total 150 days

be constantly emphasized.

In determining whether enough of the content to be assessed is being covered, it is tempting to decide that "more is better." That is not always the case, however, as shown by the curvilinear relationship between coverage and achievement for first-grade math (see Chapter 2). It is also necessary, then, to be mindful of success and to cover as much as possible without sacrificing successful performance.

Success

Two aspects of student success need to be monitored: daily work, which includes both new and review work, and unit tests. Most teachers already give students these types of assignments and keep the records in a grade book.

One simple way of monitoring daily success, in addition to the grade book, is to have each student answer one or two questions or problems on the content covered during that class period. The teacher then has a rough idea of how well the students understand that day's work. In general, the BTES-III data indicate that students should spend over half their time on work where they make few or no errors.

With respect to testing, it is perhaps best to give a unit test every 1 to 4 weeks and a review test at least every 12 weeks. Many textbooks provide unit tests at the end of each chapter, which can be used to assess student knowledge. However, it is important to remember to eliminate any items that test content not covered during instruction.

It is also important to establish standards for success or mastery of the content tested. One rule that has been used is to expect all students to do as well as the best students, which often means students should answer more than 90 percent of the questions correctly. A second rule is that students must also be able to perform the present task well enough to be able to learn future tasks. If students do not perform successfully on their first effort, it may be necessary to provide corrective feedback and additional instruction before proceeding to a new topic or unit.

One way to monitor students' success or mastery on unit tests is to develop a progress chart such as that shown in Figure A-7. Students' names are written on the side of the chart, and the skills or objectives that are to be mastered are written at the top. When a student demonstrates mastery on an objective, the date of mastery is entered for that student in the column for that objective. For example, all the students in this example have demonstrated mastery on addition and subtraction facts, regrouping, and open number sentences, but only Ann, Dave, and Harriet have done so on multiplication facts.

Figure A-7. Sample Student Progress Chart.

Student	Numeration/Place Value	Place Value to 1,000,000	Roman Numerals to 100	Add & Subtract Facts	Regrouping up to 10,000	Open Number Sentences	Multiplication Facts
Ann	9/20	9/20	9/20	9/20	10/7	10/7	10/21
Bob	9/20	9/20	9/20	9/20	10/9	10/9	
Dave	9/20	9/20	9/20	9/20	10/7	10/7	10/21
Harriet	9/21	9/21	9/21	9/21	10/7	10/7	10/21
John	9/21	9/21	9/21	9/20	10/7	10/9	
...	...	...	...	...	...	...	...
Trisha	9/20	9/20	9/20	9/20	10/9	10/9	

Appendix 2.

Policy Statement from Kent,

Washington, School District

No. 415

Effective education occurs in schools where staff, students, and parents share a desire for academic excellence, where students demonstrate high academic achievement, and where there is an equally strong degree of caring and concern for the individual.

GEORGE T. DANIEL
Superintendent, Kent School District No. 415
Kent, Washington 98031

Goals and Objectives

The Kent School District goals for 1982–83 and beyond are based on the definition of effective schools and on the recognition of our need to move toward that goal by working at the following:

1.0 Students are carefully placed in classrooms where they spend the greatest possible time actively engaged in significant learning tasks of appropriate difficulty.

    1.1 Classroom objectives are prepared which will ensure that every student is engaged in productive and appropriate activities throughout the entire period or allocated time of instruction.

    1.2 Staff demonstrates that they believe instructional time is important by planning and delivering instruction which engages all students in appropriate activity for the entire instructional period.

    1.3 Students value class time as important by being on time, by attending class, and by engaging themselves in class assignments.

2.0 Both teachers and students believe and expect that each pupil can and will perform up to high, but personally appropriate, standards of achievement and behavior.

    2.1 Administration clearly communicates district, building, grade level, and course expectations to staff.

    2.2 Staff communicates course standards and expectations to students.

    2.3 Staff accepts only the best efforts of students.

    2.4 Staff regularly evaluates students and lets them know if standards are not being met.

3.0 Student progress in achieving the established instructional goals is frequently and systematically monitored and the learning tasks are appropriately modified.

    3.1 Staff makes use of district test results to plan instruction.

    3.2 Teachers use formal and informal classroom testing to monitor and adjust instructional planning.

    3.3 Teachers use evaluation results to keep students and parents informed.

    3.4 Teachers communicate class performance to building administrators and use results to discuss instructional plans.

4.0 The school reflects a climate of being an orderly, purposeful, active, and pleasant place of well-directed, cooperative learning and interpersonal caring.

    4.1 Staff knows what is expected of them in their relationship to the total school community.

    4.2 Students know what is expected of them in being a part of the school community.

    4.3 Parents understand and support the building statements of student responsibilities and rights.

    4.4 Staff makes an effort to work together to maintain a pleasant, productive atmosphere throughout the building.

    4.5 The building reflects a feeling of success and genuine praise for achievement.

5.0 There is assertive, knowledgeable administrative leadership by the school principal, especially in regard to instruction and to creating and maintaining the four goals which precede.

5.1 Principals observe classroom instruction regularly and spend time in discussion of instructional plans and results with staff on a regular basis.

5.2 Principals are thoroughly familiar with instructional programs—objectives, materials, and activities.

5.3 Faculty meetings regularly focus on instructional goals and instructional management.

5.4 Principals use student test data to build their role as instructional leaders.

References

Abrams, J. D. "Precise Teaching Is More Effective Teaching." *Educational Leadership* 39,2 (November 1981): 138–139.

Acheson, K., and Gall, M. *Techniques in the Clinical Supervision of Teachers.* New York: Longman, Inc., 1980.

American Association of School Administrators. *Time on Task: Using Instructional Time More Effectively.* Arlington, Va.: AASA, n.d.

Anderson, L. M.; Evertson, C. M.; and Emmer, E. T. "Dimensions in Classroom Management Derived from Recent Research." Paper presented at the annual meeting of the American Educational Research Association, San Francisco, 1979.

Anderson, L. W. "Time and School Learning." Unpublished doctoral dissertation, University of Chicago, 1973.

Anderson, L. W. "Instruction and Time-on-Task: A Review." *Journal of Curriculum Studies* 13,4 (1981): 289–303.

Anderson, L. W., and Block, J. H. "Mastery Learning." In *Handbook on Teaching Educational Psychology.* Edited by D. Treffinger, J. Davis, and R. Ripple. New York: Academic Press, 1977.

Arlin, M. "Learning Rate and Learning Rate Variance Under Mastery Learning Conditions." Unpublished doctoral dissertation, University of Chicago, 1973.

Arlin, M. "Teacher Transitions Can Disrupt Time Flow in Classrooms." *American Educational Research Journal* 16,1 (1979): 42–56.

Austin, G. "Exemplary Schools and the Search for Effectiveness." *Educational Leadership* 37,1 (October 1979): 10–14.

Averch, H. A. *How Effective is Schooling? A Critical Review of Research.* Englewood Cliffs, N.J.: Educational Technology Publications, 1974.

Baily, W., and Morrill, L. "Improving Instruction Through Research-Based Staff Development." *Educational Technology* 20,9 (September 1980): 41–43.

Barber, C. "Training Principals and Teachers for Mastery Learning." *Educational Leadership* 37,2 (November 1973): 126–127.

Benjamin, R. "Towards Effective Urban Schools: A National Study." In *The Journalism Research Fellows Report: What Makes an Effective School?* Edited by D. Brundage. Washington, D.C.: George Washington University, 1979.

Berliner, D. C. *Changing Academic Learning Time: Clinical Interventions in Four Classrooms.* San Francisco, Calif.: Far West Laboratory for Educational Research and Development, 1978.

Berman, P. "Educational Change: An Implementation Paradigm." In *Improving Schools: Using What We Know.* Edited by R. Lehming and M. Kane. Beverly Hills, Calif.: Sage Publications, 1981.

Berman, P., and McLaughlin, M. W. *Federal Programs Supporting Educational Change, Vol. VIII: Factors Affecting Implementation and Continuation.* Santa Monica, Calif.: Rand Corporation, 1977.

Block, J. H. "The Effects of Various Levels of Performance on Selected Cognitive, Affective, and Time Variables." Unpublished doctoral dissertation, University of Chicago, 1970.

Block, J. H., and Burns, R. B. "Mastery Learning." In *Review of Research in Education.* Vol. 4. Edited by L. S. Schulman. Itasca, Ill.: F. E. Peacock, 1976.

Bloom, B. S. *Human Characteristics and Student Learning.* New York: McGraw-Hill, 1976.

Bracht, G. H., and Hopkins, K. D. "Stability of Educational Achievement." In *Perspectives in Educational and Psychological Measurement*. Edited by G. H. Bracht, K. D. Hopkins, and J. C. Stanley. Englewood Cliffs, N.J.: Prentice-Hall, 1972.

Brady, M. E.; Clinton, D.; Sweeney, J. M.; Peterson, M.; and Poynor, H. *Instructional Dimensions Study*. Washington, D.C.: Kirschner Associates, Inc., 1977.

Bridge, R. G.; Judd, C. M.; and Moock, P. R. *The Determinants of Educational Outcomes: The Impact of Families, Peers, Teachers, and Schools*. Cambridge, Mass.: Ballinger Publishing Company, 1979.

Brookover, W.; Beady, C.; Flood, P.; Schweitzer, J; and Wisenbaker, J. *School Social Systems and Student Achievement: Schools Can Make a Difference*. New York: Praeger, 1979.

Brundage, D., ed. *The Journalism Research Fellows Report: What Makes an Effective School?* Washington, D.C.: George Washington University, 1979.

Burns, R. B. "Mastery Learning: Does it Work?" *Educational Leadership* 37,2 (November 1979): 110–113.

Bussis, A. M.; Chittendon, E. A.; and Amarel, M. *Beyond Surface Curriculum: An Interview Study of Teacher's Understandings*. Boulder, Colo.: Westview Press, 1976.

Carroll, J. B. "A Model of School Learning." *Teachers College Record* 64 (1963): 723–733.

Champagne, D., and Hogen, C. "A Competency-Based Training Program for Middle Managers of the Educational System." *Supervisory and Management Skills* 2,2 (1978): 423–436.

Cogan, M. *Clinical Supervision*. Boston: Houghton-Mifflin, 1973.

Cohen, E. G. "Design and Redesign of the Desegregated School: Problems of Status, Power, and Conflict." In *School Desegregation: Past, Present, and Future*. Edited by W. G. Stephen and J. R. Feagin. New York: Plenum, 1980.

Coleman, J. S.; Campbell, E. Q.; Hobson, C. J.; McPartland, J.; Mood, A. M.; Weinfeld, F. D.; and York, R. L. *Equality of Educational Opportunity*. Washington, D.C.: U.S. Government Printing Office, 1966.

Cooley, W. W., and Leinhardt, G. "The Instructional Dimensions Study." *Educational Evaluation and Policy Analysis* 2,1 (1980): 7–24.

Corbett, H. D. "Principals' Contributions to Maintaining Change." *Phi Delta Kappan* 64,3 (November 1982): 190–192.

Corbett, H. *To Make an Omelet You Have to Break the Egg Crate: Teacher Interdependence Promotes School-wide Change*. Philadelphia, Pa.: Research for Better Schools, Inc., 1982.

Crain, R. *Southern Schools: An Evaluation of the Emergency School Assistance Program and of Desegregation*. Vol. 1. Chicago: National Opinion Research Center, 1973.

Crawford, J. "Interactions of Learner Characteristics with the Difficulty Level of Instruction." *Journal of Educational Psychology* 70, 4 (1978): 523–531.

Crawford, W. J.; King, C. E.; Brophy, J. E.; and Evertson, C. M. "Error Rates and Question Difficulty Related to Elementary Children's Learning." Paper presented at the annual meeting of the American Educational Research Association, Washington, D.C., April 1975.

Davey, A. "Teachers, Race, and Intelligence." *Race* 15 (1973): 195.

Davidson, J.; Hofman, G.; and Brown, W. "Measuring and Explaining High School Interracial Climates." *Social Problems* 26, 1 (1978): 50–70.

Dishaw, M. *Descriptions of Allocated Time to Content Areas for the A-B Period*. BTES Technical Note Series, Technical Note IV-2a. San Francisco: Far West Laboratory for Educational Research and Development, July 1977.

Duckett, W.; Park, D.; Clark, D.; McCarthy, M.; Lotto, L.; Gregory, L.; Herling, J.; and Burlson, D. *Why Do Some Schools Succeed? The Phi Delta Kappa Study of Exceptional Elementary Schools*. Bloomington, Ind.: Phi Delta Kappa, 1980.

Duke, D., ed. *Classroom Management: The Seventy-Eighth Yearbook of the National Society for the Study of Education*. Chicago: University of Chicago Press, 1979.

Dunn, R. S., and Dunn, K. J. "Learning Styles/Teaching Styles: Should They . . . Can They . . . Be Matched?" *Educational Leadership* 36,4 (January 1979): 238–244.

Eddy, E. *Walk the White Line*. New York: Doubleday, 1976.

Edmonds, E. "Effective Schools for the Urban Poor." *Educational Leadership* 37,1 (October 1979): 15–24.

Egerton, J. *Education and Desegregation in Eight Schools*. Amherst, Mass.: Center for Equal Education, 1977.

Ekstein, R., and Wallerstein, R. *The Teaching and Learning of Psychotherapy*. New York: Basic Books, Inc., 1958.

Ellett, C.; Pool, J.; and Hill, A. "A Time-Motion Study of Principals in Thomas County, Georgia." *CCBC Notebook* 4,1 (1974).

Emmer, E., and Evertson, C. "Synthesis of Research on Classroom Management." *Educational Leadership* 38,4 (January 1981): 342–347.

Emmer, E.; Evertson, C.; and Anderson, L. "Effective Classroom Management at the Beginning of the School Year." *Elementary School Journal* 80,5 (1980): 219–231.

Emrick, J., and Peterson, S. *A Synthesis of Findings Across Five Recent Studies of Educational Dissemination and Change*. Executive summary. San Francisco: Far West Laboratory for Educational Research and Development, 1978.

English, F. W. "Curriculum Mapping." *Educational Leadership* 37,7 (April 1980): 558–559.

Etzioni, A. *Modern Organizations*. Englewood Cliffs, N.J.: Prentice-Hall, Inc., 1964.

Felsenthal, H. "The Present: What Works in the Teaching of Reading." Paper presented at the 21st Century Expo, Madison, 1978.

Firestone, W. "Images of Schools and Patterns of Change." *American Journal of Education* 88,4 (1980): 45.

Fischer, B. B., and Fischer, L. "Styles in Teaching and Learning." *Educational Leadership* 36,4 (January 1979): 245–254.

Fisher, C. W.; Filby, N. N.; Marliave, R. S.; Cahen, L. S.; Dishaw, M. M.; Moore, J. E; and Berliner, D. C. *Teaching Behaviors, Academic Learning Time, and Student Achievement: Final Report of Phase III-B, Beginning Teacher Evaluation Study*. San Francisco: Far West Laboratory for Educational Research and Development, 1978.

Fisher, C.; Marliave, R.; and Filby, N. "Improving Teaching by Increasing 'Academic Learning Time.' " *Educational Leadership* 37,1 (October 1979): 52–54.

Floden, R. E.; Porter, A. C.; Schmidt, W. H.; and Freeman, D. J. "Don't They all Measure the Same Thing? Consequences of Standardized Test Selection." In *Educational Testing and Evaluation: Design, Analysis, and Policy*. Edited by E. L. Baker and E. S. Quellmalz. Beverly Hills, Calif.: Sage, 1980.

Floden, R. E.; Porter, A. C.; Schmidt, W. H.; Freeman, D. J.; and Schwille, J. R. "Responses to Curriculum Pressures: A Policy-Capturing Study of Teacher Decisions About Content." *Journal of Educational Psychology* 73,2 (1981): 129–141.

Freeman, D. J., and Kuhs, T. M. *The Fourth Grade Mathematics Curriculum as Inferred from Textbooks and Tests*. Paper presented at the annual meeting of the American Educational Research Association, Boston, April 1980.

Fullan, M., and Pomfret, A. "Research on Curriculum and Instruction Implementation." *Review of Educational Research* 47,2 (1977): 335–397.

Goldhammer, R. *Clinical Supervision: Special Methods for the Supervision of Teachers*. New York: Holt, Rinehart & Winston, 1969.

Goldhammer, R.; Anderson, R.; and Krajewski, R. *Clinical Supervision*. New York: Holt, Rinehart & Winston, 1980.

Goldstein, J. M., and Weber, W. A. *Teacher Managerial Behaviors and Student On-Task Behavior: Three Studies*. Paper presented at the annual meeting of the American Educational Research Association, Los Angeles, April 1981.

Good, T. L., and Grouws, D. A. "Teaching and Mathematics Learning." *Educational Leadership* 37,1 (October 1979): 39–45.

Graeber, A.; Rim, E-D; and Unks, N. *A Survey of Classroom Practices and Sixth Grade Teachers in Delaware, New Jersey, and Pennsylvania*. Philadelphia: Research for Better Schools, Inc., 1977.

Gross, D. The Supervisory Process: Multiple-Impact Supervision. In *The Counselor Handbook*. Edited by G. F. Farwell, N. F. Gamsky, and F. Mathieu-Coughlan. New York: Intext, 1974.

Hansen, J., and Warner, R. "Review of Research on Practicum Supervision." *Counselor Education and Supervision* 10 (1971): 261–273.

Havelock, R. G. *A Guide to Innovation in Education*. Ann Arbor: Institute of Social Research,

University of Michigan, 1970.

Heinrichs, A., and Rim, E-D. *A Survey of Classroom Practices in Reading: Reports of First, Third, Fourth, and Sixth Grade Teachers in Delaware, New Jersey, and Pennsylvania.* Philadelphia: Research for Better Schools, Inc., 1980.

Henderson, R. D.; Von Euler, M.; and Schneider, J. M. "Remedies for Segregation: Some Lessons from Research." *Educational Evaluation and Policy Analysis* 3,4 (1981): 67–76.

Herrick, C. "A Phenomenological Study of Supervisees' Positive and Negative Experiences in Supervision." Unpublished doctoral dissertation, University of Pittsburgh, 1977.

Horgan, J. "A Natural History Approach to the Teaching-Learning Process of Supervision: A Critical Analysis of Supervisor Strategies of Intervention in the Training of Counselors." Unpublished doctoral dissertation, University of Pittsburgh, 1971.

Huitt, W., and Segars, J. *Characteristics of Effective Classrooms.* Philadelphia, Pa.: Research for Better Schools, Inc., 1980.

Huitt, W.; Caldwell, J.; Traver, P.; and Graeber, A. "Collecting Information on Student Engaged Time." In *Time Leader's Guide.* Edited by D. Helms, A. Graeber, J. Caldwell, and W. Huitt. Philadelphia, Pa.: Research for Better Schools Inc., 1981.

Hunter, M. "Teaching is Decision-Making." *Educational Leadership* 37,1 (October 1979): 62–67.

Irvine, D. J. "Factors Associated with School Effectiveness." *Educational Technology* 29,5 (1979): 53–55.

Jones, J.; Erickson, E.; and Crowell, R. "Decreasing the Gap Between Whites and Blacks." *Education and Urban Society* 4 (1972): 339–349.

Kell, B., and Meuller, W. *Impact and Change: A Study of Counseling Relationships.* New York: Appleton-Century-Crafts, 1966.

Kounin, J. S. *Discipline and Group Management in Classrooms.* Huntington, N.Y.: Robert E. Kreiger Publishing Co., 1977.

Kounin, J. S., and Doyle, P. H. "Degree of Continuity of a Lesson's Signal System and the Task Involvement of Children." *Journal of Educational Psychology* 67,2 (1975) 159–164.

Lehming, R., and Kane, M., eds. *Improving Schools: Using What we Know.* Beverly Hills, Calif.: Sage Publications, 1981.

Leinhardt, G. "Applying a Classroom Process Model to Instructional Evaluation." *Curriculum Inquiry* 8,2 (1978): 155–176.

Leinhardt, G. "Modeling and Measuring Educational Treatment in Evaluation." *Review of Educational Research* 50,3 (1980): 393–420.

Letteri, C. A. "Cognitive Profile: Basic Determinant of Academic Achievement." *The Journal of Educational Research* 73,4 (1980): 195–198.

Levin, T. "The Effect of Content Prerequisite and Process-Oriented Experiences on Application Ability in the Learning of Probability." Unpublished doctoral dissertation, University of Chicago, 1975.

Lincoln, W. *Mediation: A Transferable Process for the Prevention and Resolution of Racial Conflict in Public Secondary Schools.* Washington, D.C.: National Institute of Education, 1976.

Lipham, J. M. "The Administrator's Role in Educational Linkage." In *Linking Processes in Educational Improvement.* Edited by N. Nash and J. Culbertson. Columbus, Ohio: University Council for Educational Administration, 1977.

Little, J. W. "School Success and Staff Development in Urban Desegregated Schools: A Summary of Recently Completed Research." Paper presented at the annual meeting of the American Educational Research Association, Los Angeles, April 1981.

Mackler, B. "Grouping in the Ghetto." *Education and Urban Society* 2 (1969): 82.

Marliave, R., and Filby, N. "A Simple Procedure for Analyzing Task Appropriateness, with Applications in Remedial Reading Instruction." Paper presented at the annual meeting of the American Educational Research Association, Boston, April 1980.

McLaughlin, M. W., and Marsh, D. D. "Staff Development and School Change." *Teachers College Record* 80,1 (1978): 69–94.

Medley, D. M. *Teacher Competence and Teacher Effectiveness.* Washington, D.C.: American Association of Colleges for Teacher Evaluation, 1977.

Naegley, R., and Evans, D. *Handbook for Effective Supervision of Instruction.* Englewood

Cliffs, N.J.: Prentice-Hall, 1980.

Noblit, G. "Patience and Prudence in a Southern High School." In *Desegregated Schools.* Edited by R. Rist. New York: Academic Press, 1979.

Ozecelik, D. A. "Student Involvement in the Learning Process." Unpublished doctoral dissertation, University of Chicago, 1974.

Peterson, P. L.; Marx, R. W.; and Clark, C. M. "Teacher Planning, Teacher Behavior, and Student Achievement." *American Educational Research Journal* 15,3 (1978): 417–432.

Pettes, D. *Supervision in Social Work.* London: George Allen and Unwin Ltd., 1967.

Pettigrew, T. "The Cold Structural Inducements to Integration." *Urban Review* 8 (1975): 137–144.

Pincus, J., and Williams, R. C. "Planned Change in Urban School Districts." *Phi Delta Kappan* 60,10 (June 1979): 729–733.

Porwoll, P. *Class Size.* Arlington, Va.: Educational Research Service, 1978.

Reinhard, D. L.; Arends, R. A.; Kutz, W.; Lovell, K.; and Wyant, S. "Great Expectations: The Principal's Role and Inservice Needs in Supporting Change Projects." Paper presented at the annual meeting of the American Educational Research Association, Boston, April 1980.

Rim, E-D. Personal communication, 1980.

Rim, E-D.; Caldwell, J.; Helms, D.; and Huitt, W. "Comparing Student Engaged Time to Research Data." In *Time Leader's Guide.* Edited by D. Helms, A. Graeber, J. Caldwell, and W. Huitt. Philadelphia, Pa.: Research for Better Schools, Inc., 1981.

Rist, R. *The Invisible Children.* Cambridge, Mass.: Harvard University Press, 1978.

Rist, R., ed. *Desegregated Schools.* New York: Academic Press, 1979.

Rosenshine, B. V. *Primary Grades Instruction and Student Achievement Gain.* Urbana, Ill.: Bureau of Educational Research, 1977.

Rosenshine, B. V. "Content, Time, and Direct Instruction." In *Research on Teaching: Concepts, Findings and Implications.* Edited by P. L. Peterson and J. J. Walbert. Berkeley, Calif.: McCutchan Publishing Corp., 1979.

Rosenshine, B., and Furst, N. "The Use of Direct Observation to Study Teaching." In *Second Handbook of Research on Teaching.* Edited by R. M. W. Traver. Chicago: Rand McNally & Co., 1973.

Runkel, P. J., and Schmuck, R. A. "Findings from the Research and Development Program on Strategies of Organizational Change at CEPM-CASEA." Unpublished paper, Center for Educational Policy and Management, University of Oregon, Eugene, 1974.

Rutter, M.; Maughan, B.; Mortimore, P.; Ouston, J.; and Smith, A. *Fifteen Thousand Hours: Secondary Schools and Their Effects on Children.* Cambridge: Harvard University Press, 1979.

Ryan, D., and Hickcox, E. *Redefining Teacher Evaluation.* Toronto, Ontario: Ontario Institute for Studies in Education, 1980.

Schofield, J. *The Impact of Positively Structured Schooling on Intergroup Behavior.* Washington, D.C.: National Institute of Education, 1978.

Schuster, D.; Standt, J.; and Thaler, D. *Clinical Supervision and the Psychiatric Resident.* New York: Brunner/Mazel, 1972.

Segars, J.; Caldwell, J.; Graeber, A.; and Huitt, W. "Collecting Information on Prior Learning and Instructional Overlap." In *Content Leader's Guide.* Edited by D. Helms, A. Graeber, J. Caldwell, and J. Segars. Philadelphia, Pa.: Research for Better Schools, 1981.

Shavelson, R., and Stern, P. "Research on Teachers' Pedagogical Thoughts, Judgments, Decisions, and Behavior." *Review of Educational Research* 51, 4 (1981):455–498.

Sikorski, L. A.; Turnbull, B. J.; Thorn, L. I.; and Bell, S. R. *Factors Influencing School Change.* San Francisco: Far West Laboratory for Educational Research and Development, 1976. (ERIC Document No. ED 129 622.)

Skinner, B. F. *The Technology of Teaching.* New York: Appleton-Century-Crofts, 1968.

Soar, R. S., and Soar, R. M. "Emotional Climate and Teacher Management: A Paradigm and Some Results." In *Conceptions of Teaching.* Edited by H. S. Walberg and P. L. Peterson. Berkeley, Calif.: National Society for the Study of Education and McCutchan Publishing Corp., 1977.

Squires, D. "A Phenomenological Study of Supervisors' Perception of a Positive Supervisory Experience." Unpublished doctoral dissertation, University of Pittsburgh, 1978.

Squires, D. *Characteristics of Effective Schools: The Importance of School Processes.* Philadelphia: Research for Better Schools, Inc., 1980. (ERIC Document No. ED 197 486.)

Squires, D. "The Meaning and Structure of a Positive Supervisory Experience from a Supervisor's Perspective." Paper presented at the annual meeting of the American Educational Research Association, Los Angeles, April 1981.

Squires, D. A., and Huitt, W. G. "Supervision for Effective Classrooms: Five Phases of a Positive Supervisory Experience." Paper presented at the annual meeting of the Association for Supervision and Curriculum Development, St. Louis, March 1981.

Squires, D.; Huitt, W.; and Segars, J. "Improving Classrooms and Schools: What's Important." *Educational Leadership* 39,3 (December 1981): 174–179.

Stallings, J. A., and Kaskowitz, D. *Follow Through Classroom Observation Evaluation, 1972–1973.* Menlo Park, Calif.: Stanford Research Institute, 1974.

Stout, R. T. and Rowe, A. D. "Differential Success of Organization Development in Schools: A Comparative Analysis." Paper presented at the annual meeting of the American Educational Research Association, Los Angeles, April 1981.

Sullivan, C. *Clinical Supervision.* Alexandria, Va.: Association for Supervision and Curriculum Development, 1980.

U.S. Department of Health, Education, and Welfare. *Violent Schools—Safe Schools: The Safe School Study Report to the Congress, Volume I.* Washington, D.C.: Government Printing Office, 1978.

Vann, A. "Three Principals Discuss the Principal's Leadership Role. Can Principals Lead in Curriculum Development?" *Educational Leadership* 36,6 (March 1979): 404–405.

Weber, G. *Inner-City Children Can be Taught to Read: Four Successful Schools.* CBE Occasional Papers, No. 18. Washington, D.C.: Council for Basic Education, 1971.

Weick, K. "Educational Organizations as Loosely Coupled Systems." *Administrative Science Quarterly* 21,1 (1976): 1–19.

Weiss, I. R. *Report of the 1977 National Survey of Science, Mathematics, and Social Studies Education.* Washington, D.C.: U.S. Government Printing Office, 1978.

Wellisch, J. B.; MacQueen, A. H.; Carriere, R. A.; and Duck, F. A. "School Management and Organization in Successful Schools." *Sociology of Education* 51 (1978): 211, 226.

Wiley, D. E., and Harnischfeger, A. "Explosion of a Myth: Quantity of Schooling and Exposure to Instruction, Major Educational Vehicles." *Educational Researcher* 4,3 (1974): 7–11.

Willie, C., and Greenblatt, S. *Community Politics and Educational Change: Ten School Systems Under Court Order.* New York: Longman, 1980.

Zahorik, J. "Teachers' planning models." *Educational Leadership* 33,2 (November 1975):134–139.

Zaltman, G.; Florio, D.; and Sikorski, L. *Dynamic Educational Change.* New York: The Free Press, 1977.

About the Authors

David A. Squires is Supervisor of Curriculum and Staff Development, Red Bank Borough Schools, Red Bank, New Jersey.

William G. Huitt is Instructor, Psychology and Education, Navajo Community College, Tsaile, Arizona.

John K. Segars is Director of Staff Development, Pee Dee Regional Education Center, Florence, South Carolina.

The authors previously worked with Research for Better Schools, Inc., Philadelphia, Pennsylvania.

Also of interest . . .

For further exploration of school and classroom effectiveness, readers may find the following ASCD media useful:

Publications

	Price	Quantity
Effective Instruction. Tamar Levin and Ruth Long. Suggests methods to help teachers improve student learning and achievement. 1981. 102 pp. 611-80212.	$6.50	_____
School Effectiveness, Teacher Effectiveness. Theme issue of *Educational Leadership*. October 1979. 96 pp. 611-79170.	$2.00	_____

Audiocassettes

The Characteristics of Schools That Are Instructionally Effective for All Pupils. Ronald Edmonds. Reports school effectiveness research and describes New York City's effective schools project. 1981. 73 mins. 612-20234.	$9.00	_____
Research on Effective Schools and Effective Teachers: Strategies for Implementation in Local Schools. Thomas L. McGreal. Describes how school districts are using effectiveness research to improve their schools. 1983. 70 mins. 612-20322.	$9.00	_____
Research on Effective Schools. Lawrence W. Lezotte. Explains the process Lezotte and his colleagues use to identify instructionally effective schools. 1983. 75 mins. 612-20368.	$9.00	_____

Videotape

Teacher and School Effectiveness. Ronald Edmonds, Barak Rosenshine, and Peter Mortimore, featured educators. Three noted researchers explain how their studies were conducted, summarize their findings, and suggest how schools can use the results to improve their own programs. 21 mins.

Format (specify no. of copies)
¾" cassette _____
½" reel _____
½" Beta _____
½" VHS _____

Rental ($50 for five days)
Preferred date _____
Alternate date _____
Unscheduled preview ($30 for two days) _____

Purchase
ASCD members, $195 _____
Nonmembers, $230 _____

Ordering and Payment Information

1. Indicate on the form the quantity of each item you wish to order.
2. Please be sure your name and address appear below.
3. All orders totaling $20 or less must be accompanied by payment. ASCD absorbs the cost of postage and handling on all prepaid orders. Make check or money order payable to ASCD.
4. If order is to be billed, postage and handling are extra.
5. Orders from institutions and businesses must be on an official purchase order form.

Mail to:
ASCD
225 N. Washington St.
Alexandria, VA 22314
(703) 549-9110

Please check form of payment:
_____ Enclosed is my check or money order in the amount of $ _____
_____ Please bill me (postage and handling extra)

Name _____

Address _____

_____

City _____ **State** _____ **Zip** _____